T0095897

BIRMINGHAM CITY
On This Day

BIRMINGHAM CITY
On This Day

*History, Facts & Figures
from Every Day of the Year*

TIM EVERSHED

BIRMINGHAM CITY
On This Day
History, Facts & Figures
from Every Day of the Year

All statistics, facts and figures are correct as of 1st July 2017

© Tim Evershed

Tim Evershed has asserted his rights in accordance with the Copyright, Designs and Patents Act 1988 to be identified as the author of this work.

Published By:
Pitch Publishing (Brighton) Ltd
A2 Yeoman Gate
Yeoman Way
Durrington
BN13 3QZ

Email: info@pitchpublishing.co.uk
Web: www.pitchpublishing.co.uk

Published 2017

A catalogue record for this book is available from the British Library

ISBN 9781785313080

Typesetting and origination by Pitch Publishing
Printed in Great Britain by TJ International

DEDICATION

For Hayley

FOREWORD

Birmingham City's club anthem reminds its supporters of the sacred contract to which they have agreed.

The words to *Keep Right On* not only hint at long-suffering and forbearance, they actually exhort Blue hearts to beat strong.

And for every 'joy' contained in Tim Evershed's *Year in the life of a Bluenose*, there's a 'sorrow' to go with it. This book is a reminder of the travails of being a Birmingham City fan.

But perhaps the dominant message in these pages is one of defiant pride. No matter how tired and weary Blues feel they always bounce back. There is always another day.

As if to prove that point even after 140 years of history their most recent match was a gutsy and determined victory at Bristol City. It saved their Championship status and neatly summarised the rollercoaster ride that is following the club that bears the Second City's name. This extensively researched book does likewise.

Brian Dick
Birmingham City Correspondent – Birmingham Mail

INTRODUCTION

Birmingham City On This Day chronicles the club's history in terms of the facts, figures and trivia that have occurred on each day of the calendar year.

The club has had an eventful history on and off the pitch with highs and lows stretching back over 140 years. Anyone reading this book from start to finish will be fed that history in a seemingly random and haphazard manner as it zips back and forth throughout that time.

Nevertheless, I have endeavoured to include the important events and key characters that have shaped the club and its history. I also hope that there is more than a smattering of interesting anecdotes and enlightening tales for Blues fans everywhere.

Happy reading.

ACKNOWLEDGEMENTS

The writing of this book would not have been possible without the work of the journalists, historians and authors who have documented the story and results of Birmingham City. I owe a debt of gratitude to Tony Matthews, Andrew Henry, Keith Dixon, Tom Ross, Colin Tattum, Peter Lewis, Brian Dick and many more.

My thanks also goes to Wayne Cowen at Birmingham City for his assistance.

I would also like to extend my heartfelt thanks to me proofing team of Ruth Cassidy, David Evershed, Darryl Smith, Lawrence Telford and Susie Wyeth for their diligent efforts.

Finally, thanks to my wife Hayley and sons William and Joseph for their love and support.

BIRMINGHAM CITY
On This Day

JANUARY

TUESDAY 1st JANUARY 1985

A spell of four goals in 16 second-half minutes turned Birmingham City's match at Sheffield United on its head. After a goalless first half at Bramall Lane the Blades had taken a 2-0 lead and looked on course for victory. However, a 62nd minute Robert Hopkins volley started a remarkable comeback. Dave Geddis levelled the scores with his fourth goal in as many games before Wayne Clarke and a Gary West own goal put City in command. Although United's Colin Morris won and converted a penalty the match finished 4-3 to Blues.

THURSDAY 1st JANUARY 1987

Blues started the New Year with a 3-2 win over Plymouth Argyle but victory was marred by a horror injury to debutant Paul Hart. The defender suffered a broken leg in an accidental collision with team-mate Tommy Williams that ended his playing career. Blues overcame the shock of Hart's injury to defeat Plymouth at St Andrew's with Martin Kuhl, Wayne Clarke and Dennis Mortimer getting the Birmingham goals.

WEDNESDAY 1st JANUARY 2003

Jasper Carrott was appointed to the Order of the British Empire in the New Year's Honours List for 'his charitable services'. Carrott was a director of Birmingham City between 1979 and 1982 and has a suite named in his honour at St Andrew's.

MONDAY 2nd JANUARY 1978

A superb Trevor Francis solo goal earned Blues a 2-1 victory over Manchester United at Old Trafford. In the 52nd minute with the scores locked at 1-1 Francis picked up the ball and slalomed past three United defenders before putting a fierce shot beyond the reach of Paddy Roche. Earlier Kevin Dillon had given City the lead and former Blue Jimmy Greenhoff had levelled for United.

MONDAY 2nd JANUARY 1995

Blues set a new club record with a 1-1 draw at Bradford City that made it 20 games unbeaten in the league and 23 matches since the team had suffered a defeat in any competition.

TUESDAY 2nd JANUARY 2003

French World Cup winner Christophe Dugarry arrived at St Andrew's on loan from Bordeaux. The striker's presence helped galvanise Steve Bruce's team as they sought to secure Premier League status. A run of five goals in four games, which all ended in victories, helped Birmingham to a 13th place finish on their return to the top flight and earned Dugarry a permanent deal with Blues.

MONDAY 3rd JANUARY 2000

Blues got the new millennium off to a winning start with a 1-0 win over Huddersfield Town in the First Division. It took midfielder Bryan Hughes just three minutes to become the first City player to score in the 21st century.

MONDAY 4th JANUARY 2016

Teenage starlet Demarai Gray departed St Andrew's after Premier League Leicester City triggered the £3.7m release clause in his contract. Gray had burst into the Birmingham team as a 17-year-old making his debut against Millwall and scoring against Blackburn Rovers soon afterwards. The following season he made 43 appearances and scored six times, three of which came in the first half of a 6-1 demolition of Reading United at St Andrew's. His performances alerted a host of Premier League clubs, including Liverpool and Tottenham Hotspur, but it was the Foxes who won the race for the young winger's signature.

SATURDAY 5th JANUARY 1895

Small Heath's first Football League meeting with Blackburn Rovers ended in a disastrous 9-1 defeat at Ewood Park and a horror debut for keeper Tilson Pritchard. Ted Killean and Henry Chippendale both scored hat-tricks for the home side while Billy Walton got Blues' consolation goal. The eight-goal margin remains the equal heaviest defeat in club history.

SATURDAY 5th JANUARY 1918

Guest player Danny Shea was amongst the goals as Blues and Notts County drew 3-3 in a wartime match. Five years earlier Blackburn Rovers had broken the transfer record for Shea paying West Ham United £2,000 for his services.

WEDNESDAY 6th JANUARY 1915

Blues romped to one of the biggest victories in their history with an 11-1 demolition of Glossop in the Second Division. Forwards Jimmy Windridge and Andy Smith scored nine goals between them with the former getting five, including a penalty. Frank Hodges and Edmund Eyre scored a goal each as Birmingham ran riot.

SATURDAY 7th JANUARY 1893

Charlie Simms made his one and only Football League appearance for Small Heath after Caesar Jenkyns missed his train to the match at Lincoln City. Blues overcame both the loss of Jenkyns and the bitterly cold weather to beat Lincoln City 4-3. Snow had to be cleared off the pitch before kick-off then a late Freddie Wheldon hat-trick and a Tommy Hands strike gave Blues victory.

SATURDAY 7th JANUARY 1922

The first round proper of the FA Cup took place with 32 ties played across England and Wales. However, the name of Birmingham City was missing from the fixture list due to an administrative error. Secretary-manager Frank Richards had failed to submit the relevant paperwork on time. Richards said: 'It was just one of those things – it could have happened even in the best-regulated families.'

SATURDAY 7th JANUARY 1956

Birmingham City thrashed Torquay United 7-1 at Plainmoor in the third round of the FA Cup. It was the first away trip as Blues made it all the way to the FA Cup Final without playing a single home fixture. Eddie Brown scored a hat-trick to lead the destruction of Torquay with Peter Murphy adding two goals while Noel Kinsey and Gordon Astall scored one apiece.

FRIDAY 7th JANUARY 1994

Blues manager Barry Fry brought Steve Claridge to the club from Cambridge United in a £350,000 deal. The 1994/95 season was Claridge's only full season at the club and he top scored with 25 goals in all competitions, helping fire Blues to the lower league double of the Second Division title and Football League Trophy.

SATURDAY 8th JANUARY 1994

Blues were victims of an FA Cup giant-killing, as they were beaten 2-1 at St Andrew's by non-league Kidderminster Harriers. Paul Harding gave Birmingham an early lead but a close range Neil Cartwright header levelled the scores before John Purdie struck a fine winner in the 64th minute. Blues dominated the game but Andy Saville missed a penalty and a late goal was ruled out.

SATURDAY 9th JANUARY 1954

Birmingham City sprang an FA Cup shock as they dumped double-chasing Wolverhampton Wanderers out of the FA Cup in the third round. Wolves, who went on to win their first league title, took an early lead at Molineux through England international Dennis Wilshaw. City's Ken Rowley levelled the scores two minutes later and although the visitors rode their luck, twice they were saved by the woodwork, Peter Murphy's second-half strike sent the Second Division Blues through to the next round.

SATURDAY 10th JANUARY 1903

Bad light caused Small Heath's match at Manchester City to be abandoned in the 83rd minute with Blues leading 1-0. The Citizens won the re-scheduled fixture 4-0 the following month.

SATURDAY 10th JANUARY 1931

A comfortable 2-0 victory over Liverpool in the third round of the FA Cup began Birmingham City's journey on a road that would lead all the way to Wembley and a first appearance in the FA Cup Final. Joe Bradford and Ernie Curtis scored the goals that ensured Blues' safe passage into the next round.

SATURDAY 10th JANUARY 1998

Blues equalled their biggest away victory in the Football League with a 7-0 win at Stoke City. Two Bryan Hughes goals in the opening ten minutes set City on course for a convincing win on their second visit to the Britannia Stadium. Paul Furlong scored a hat-trick while Nicky Forster and Jon McCarthy were also on the score-sheet. The goal spree equalled the score-line from Blues' victory at Northwich Victoria set 104 years earlier.

TUESDAY 11th JANUARY 1955

Joe Gallagher was born in Liverpool, Merseyside. The centre-half made his Blues debut in 1972 at the age of 17 and was first named as captain of the side before reaching his 20th birthday. In 11 years Gallagher played 335 matches and scored 23 goals for Blues earning himself a testimonial match against Aston Villa in the process. In 1981 Gallagher was transferred to Wolverhampton Wanderers for £350,000, although Blues never saw most of the transfer fee after the Molineux club was declared bankrupt.

SATURDAY 12th JANUARY 1946

A bumper crowd of 63,280 was at Villa Park to see Blues secure another point along the way to winning the wartime Football League South title. Welsh international Don Dearson and inside-right Neil Dougall scored Birmingham's goals while goalkeeper Gil Merrick denied Villa's Harry Parkes from the penalty spot to earn a 2-2 draw. A week later a 3-1 victory for City in the return fixture at St Andrew's would prove vital as City squeezed out Villa for the last wartime title on goal average.

WEDNESDAY 12th JANUARY 1994

Arthur Turner died in Sheffield, South Yorkshire aged 84. The centre-half joined Blues from Stoke City in 1939 for £6,000. He made over 160 wartime appearances for Birmingham City, including captaining the side that won the League South title and reached the FA Cup semi-finals in 1946. He returned to St Andrew's as manager in November 1954 and led Blues to the Second Division title that season. Turner followed that success with arguably the best season in the club's history with a 6th place finish in the top flight and an appearance in the FA Cup Final.

SUNDAY 13th JANUARY 1924

Fred Wheldon died in Worcester aged 54. The inside-forward scored twice on his Small Heath debut in a Football Alliance match against Darwen in February 1890. In all Wheldon played six seasons for Blues scoring 82 Football League and FA Cup goals in 129 appearances. Wheldon, who also played cricket for Worcestershire, was transferred to Aston Villa for £350 in June 1896.

SATURDAY 13th JANUARY 1940

A bomb-damaged St Andrew's was unable to host football so Blues were forced to entertain Leicester City on neutral ground in the wartime Midland Regional League. The match, played at Leamington's The Windmill Ground, finished 3-3.

SATURDAY 14th JANUARY 1928

Joe Bradford's second-half hat-trick saved Blues from a humiliating FA Cup exit at the hands of non-league Peterborough & Fletton United. Although City had taken an early lead through Welsh international Stan Davies the visitors, who had brought 4,000 fans to St Andrew's, led 3-1 at half-time. Les Bruton was twice on hand to take advantage of goalkeeping errors and Charles McGuigan added a third to raise the spectre of an upset. However, Blues roared back in the second half with Bradford's treble completing a remarkable comeback.

TUESDAY 14th JANUARY 1986

First Division Birmingham City were sent tumbling out of the FA Cup by non-league Altrincham. Blues ran into former keeper Jeff Wealands who made a number of saves to help the minnows to a 2-1 victory.

SATURDAY 15th JANUARY 1983

Keith Fahey was born in Dublin, Ireland. The midfielder joined Blues from Irish side St Patrick's Athletic in 2009. Fahey became a fixture in the side that gained promotion that season scoring vital goals against Southampton and Reading. He made 58 appearances over the two following seasons in the Premier League and was a member of the team that won the 2011 League Cup. Fahey stayed with Blues after they returned to the Championship and won the Goal of the Season award for his strike against Crystal Palace.

SATURDAY 16th JANUARY 1892

Small Heath's first competitive meeting with Woolwich Arsenal ended in a comprehensive 5-1 win for Blues in the FA Cup first round. Small Heath were in sparkling form with Jack Hallam and Freddie Wheldon scoring two goals each and Billy Walton made it five. The score remains the club's best result against Arsenal.

THURSDAY 16th JANUARY 1986

Blues manager Ron Saunders left the club two days after the FA Cup shock defeat at the hands of Altrincham. Saunders had become the first ex-Aston Villa boss to take charge at St Andrew's when he arrived in February 1982, shortly after his sudden departure from Villa Park. As well as going out of the cup to non-league opposition Saunders left City at the wrong end of the First Division table.

TUESDAY 17th JANUARY 1967

A disastrous first leg of the League Cup semi-final saw Blues go down 4-1 to Queens Park Rangers leaving them a mountain to climb. Although Barry Bridges gave Blues the lead after just four minutes, a second-half onslaught from Rangers saw Rodney Marsh, Roger Morgan, Mark Lazarus and Les Allen sway the tie decisively to the visitors' advantage. Forced to chase the game in the return leg at Loftus Road the Blues went down 3-1 with Eric Barber getting the City goal.

FRIDAY 18th JANUARY 2008

Blues boss Alex McLeish broke the club's transfer record when he signed Everton forward James McFadden for £4.75m. The Scot scored four goals in what remained of the 2007/08 season but it was not enough to save the club from the drop. Another four goals the following campaign helped Blues bounce back to the top flight at the first opportunity and McFadden scored the first goal on City's return to the Premier League. His final two seasons at St Andrew's were disrupted by an injury to his anterior cruciate ligament and McFadden returned to Everton on a free transfer once his contract expired in 2011. McFadden scored 14 goals in 88 appearances in all competitions for Blues

SATURDAY 19th JANUARY 1907

Aston Villa's first visit to St Andrew's attracted a huge crowd to Birmingham City's new home. Estimates for the size of the crowd vary between 45,000 and 60,000. On the pitch Blues took the spoils with a 3-2 win in a First Division fixture. Right-back Jack Glover, inside-forwards Benny Green and Arthur Mounteney scored the Blues goals.

SATURDAY 19th JANUARY 1952

Peter Murphy enjoyed a dream start to his Blues career with a hat-trick on debut. Murphy scored his first goal after just 11 minutes to set Birmingham City on course for a convincing 5-0 win against Doncaster Rovers. The inside-left, who had arrived from Tottenham Hotspur earlier in the week in a £20,000 deal, added a second shortly before half-time and completed his hat-trick in the 70th minute.

WEDNESDAY 19th JANUARY 2005

Midfielder Robbie Savage completed his controversial £3m move to Blackburn Rovers after claiming he wanted to be closer to his parents in Wrexham. Savage's claim was widely ridiculed after it transpired that Birmingham is actually two miles closer to the Welsh town than Blackburn. Birmingham owner David Sullivan said: 'We fully sympathise with Robbie if he needs to be nearer his family home. We have offered a chauffeur-driven car to take him to Wrexham any time he wants. But it's quite amusing to hear Birmingham is closer to Wrexham than Blackburn.' Although reluctant to let the midfielder go Blues at least made a profit on Savage who cost £1.25m from Leicester City.

SATURDAY 20th JANUARY 1900

Centre forward Bob McRoberts scored a hat-trick as Small Heath beat Gainsborough Trinity 8-1 to record their biggest win of the 1900/01 Second Division season. Left-half George Layton scored twice with Sid Wharton, Billy Bennett and Walter Main grabbed a goal each in the rout.

FRIDAY 20th JANUARY 1905

Birmingham City won the Birmingham Senior Cup in style with a 7-2 thrashing of West Bromwich Albion in the final at Muntz Street. Tommy Jones and Jimmy Windridge both scored hat-tricks against the Baggies with Charles Field scoring the other goal.

SATURDAY 20th JANUARY 2007

Don Weston died in Mansfield, Nottinghamshire aged 70. The centre-forward joined Blues from Wrexham for £15,000 in January 1960. He played 25 times for Birmingham, including appearances in both legs of the 1960 Inter-Cities Fairs Cup final against Barcelona.

SATURDAY 21st JANUARY 1978

Blues shocked reigning English and European champions Liverpool with a 3-2 win at Anfield. Three goals in 22 minutes after the break gave Birmingham a commanding lead on Merseyside. Trevor Francis and Keith Bertschin combined to create the opener for Welsh midfielder Gary Emmanuel. Bertschin doubled the lead three minutes later and in the 67th minute Francis won and converted a penalty to make it 3-0. A late Liverpool siege yielded goals for Phil Thompson and Kenny Dalglish, but in the final minute Blues keeper Jim Montgomery denied Jimmy Case and the team held on for a famous triumph.

TUESDAY 22nd JANUARY 1901

Joe Bradford was born in Peggs Green, Leicestershire. Bradford joined Blues in 1920 and over the next 12 years rewrote the club's goal scoring records. He hit the back of the net 267 times, including 13 hat-tricks, in 445 appearances to make him Blues' all-time leading marksman. He was top scorer in the league in all but one of his seasons at City, helping the club gain promotion in 1921, and scoring Birmingham's goal in the 1931 FA Cup Final. Bradford also scored seven England goals in just 12 appearances for his country.

WEDNESDAY 23rd JANUARY 1991

Blues boss Dave Mackay resigned after a dire run of results in the Third Division culminated in a 3-0 home defeat to John Beck's Cambridge United. The loss raised the real possibility of relegation to the fourth tier of the Football League for the first time in the club's history. Mackay had been appointed to replace Garry Pendrey in April 1989 following relegation from the Second Division. His first season in charge saw the side finish 7th but after winning their first four matches of the 1990/91 campaign the side began to struggle and Mackay was unable to halt a worrying slide down the table.

SATURDAY 24th JANUARY 1931

Joe Bradford's double strike saw off the challenge of Port Vale in the fourth round of the FA Cup as Blues moved a step closer to a first Wembley visit.

SATURDAY 24th JANUARY 1970

Mark Yates was born in Birmingham. The midfielder progressed through the youth system at St Andrew's before turning professional in 1988. He spent three seasons with Birmingham City making 68 first team appearances, including one at Wembley in the side that won the 1991 Leyland-DAF Cup, before he was sold to Burnley for £40,000 in August that year.

SATURDAY 25th JANUARY 1947

Blues progressed to the fifth round of the FA Cup at the expense of Portsmouth thanks to a Jimmy Harris goal. Blues goalkeeper Gil Merrick secured the win with a fine penalty save to deny Duggie Reid.

SATURDAY 26th JANUARY 1946

Jock Mulraney scored two goals within 70 seconds and almost added a third a minute later as Watford were thrashed 5-0 in the FA Cup fourth round. Mulraney rattled both posts with a shot that would have completed one of the quickest hat-tricks in FA Cup history. The Scottish striker did complete his treble in the second half while Harold Bodle and Wilson Jones also scored against the Hornets.

SATURDAY 26th JANUARY 1957

Alex Govan's fourth hat-trick of the season helped fire a rampant Blues side into the fifth round of the FA Cup as they thrashed Southend United 6-1 at Roots Hall. Peter Murphy got Birmingham off to a flying start with a 4th minute goal and Jimmy Lawler's own goal doubled the lead shortly afterwards. Govan added two quick goals to make it 4-0 at the break. He completed his hat-trick in the 78th minute after Geoff Cox had scored City's fifth goal.

TUESDAY 27th JANUARY 1998

Striker Paul Furlong scored his second hat-trick in three league games as Blues comfortably saw off Stockport County 4-1. It was City's second win in three days over the Hatters, after they had knocked them out of the FA Cup on the previous Saturday. Jon McCarthy scored Blues' other goal while Stockport's miserable evening was compounded by Tom Bennett's double leg fracture.

SATURDAY 28th JANUARY 1956

Blues' march to Wembley continued with a convincing 4-1 win over Leyton Orient in the fourth round of the FA Cup at Brisbane Road. Two goals from Eddie Brown and one apiece for Peter Murphy and Bill Finney saw the Blues safely into the next round.

MONDAY 28th JANUARY 1985

Future Blues player and manager Steve Bruce scored the only goal of the game as Norwich City knocked Birmingham out of the FA Cup at the fourth attempt.

SATURDAY 29th JANUARY 1972

The goal-scoring form of Trevor Francis and Bob Latchford continued as Swindon Town were swept aside 4-1 at St Andrew's. The result also extended the Blues' unbeaten run at home to a 28 matches. Francis opened the scoring against Swindon with stunning volley that was his sixth goal in as many games. Latchford added two more, on his way to 30 goals for the season, with Bob Hatton also on target.

SATURDAY 30th JANUARY 1892

Small Heath travelled to Sheffield Wednesday despite having been drawn first out of the hat in the FA Cup. The club accepted Wednesday's offer of £200 to play the tie at the Olive Grove instead of hosting the game. A rough match on a windy day saw the home side reduced to nine men as two Wednesday players were sent off for punching and kicking. The Owls made light of their numerical disadvantage to win 2-0.

SATURDAY 30th JANUARY 1954

Birmingham City tumbled out of the FA Cup to Third Division (South) side Ipswich Town with Welsh international Billy Reed scoring the only goal of the game.

TUESDAY 30th JANUARY 1996

Blues exited the Anglo-Italian Cup after losing 4-1 in a penalty shoot-out to West Bromwich Albion at The Hawthorns. Former Blue Dave Smith scored the winning penalty for the Baggies after the match finished 2-2.

TUESDAY 31st JANUARY 1995

Paul Tait's golden goal secured Blues' passage into the southern area final of the Auto-Windscreens Shields Trophy. Birmingham and Swansea City had finished the 90 minutes locked together at 2-2. Colin Pascoe gave the Welsh side an early lead that was cancelled out by Steve Claridge. An unfortunate Kenny Lowe own goal restored the visitors' lead at St Andrew's before £800,000 signing Kevin Francis put Blues on level terms once again. Seven minutes into extra time Tait struck to send City through.

WEDNESDAY 31st JANUARY 2001

Extra-time goals from record signing Geoff Horsfield and Andy Johnson booked Blues their place in a first major final for 45 years. Birmingham City were trailing Ipswich Town 1-0 after the first leg of the League Cup semi-final but made it through to Cardiff after a raucous night at St Andrew's in front of 28,264 fans. Martin Grainger scored just before the break to level the tie and Horsfield scored at the second attempt to give the home side the lead. Ipswich hit back a minute later through Jamie Scowcroft and the 90 minutes ended with the tie all-square at 2-2. Horsfield restored Blues' lead in the first period of extra time after latching onto Danny Sonner's brilliant through ball. Then Johnson pounced on a goalkeeping error to score into an open goal and send City through to the first League Cup final to be held at the Millennium Stadium.

TUESDAY 31st JANUARY 2012

Giant Serb Nikola Zigic put all of his 6ft 8in height to good use as he scored three times with his head in the process of grabbing all four Birmingham goals in a 4-1 win over Leeds United. Zigic's second, third and fourth goals came within the space of seven minutes to equal a club record set 44 years earlier by Phil Summerill. A bullet header from Zigic levelled the scores at half-time after Scotland striker Ross McCormack had given Leeds the lead. Then a devastating spell saw Blues' record signing grab three goals between the 61st and 68th minutes to emphatically decide the outcome of the match.

BIRMINGHAM CITY
On This Day

FEBRUARY

SATURDAY 1st FEBRUARY 1941

Walter Abbott died in Birmingham aged 63. The inside-left holds the Blues record for goals in a season with 42 during the 1898/99 campaign. It was the second season in succession that Abbott top scored for Blues and 34 of his goals came in the league at the rate of one per game. His feats in front of goal earned him a move to Everton where he won an England cap. Abbott scored 66 goals in 85 Blues appearances in all competitions.

SATURDAY 1st FEBRUARY 1986

Birmingham City finally won a league match at the 18th attempt as Wayne Clarke's goal was enough to see off Oxford United 1-0 at the Manor Ground. The 17-match winless streak dated back to the previous September and Blues had exited both cup competitions as well as slumping in the league during this barren period.

FRIDAY 2nd FEBRUARY 2001

Blues signed Sheffield United midfielder Curtis Woodhouse for £1m. Woodhouse made his debut the following day in a 2-1 win over Norwich City at St Andrew's. A goal in each half from Bryan Hughes and Darren Purse helped continue Birmingham City's promotion push and consigned the Canaries to their 10th away defeat of the season. Woodhouse played 45 times for Birmingham, scoring two goals. After spells with Peterborough United, Hull City and Grimsby Town the midfielder retired from football and became a professional boxer. He went on to win 22 professional bouts, 13 by knockout, and briefly held the British Light-Welterweight title.

SATURDAY 2nd FEBRUARY 1980

Ten-man Blues held on for a 1-0 victory against Charlton Athletic at The Valley after midfielder Colin Todd had seen red in the 56th minute. Birmingham led in London thanks to Archie Gemmill's 36th minute strike and hung on for the win despite the numerical disadvantage.

SATURDAY 3rd FEBRUARY 1962

Bertie Auld scored Blues' consolation goal as they were thumped 7-1 by Burnley at Turf Moor.

THURSDAY 4th FEBRUARY 1904

Bob Gregg was born in Ferryhill, County Durham. The inside-forward joined Birmingham City from Sheffield Wednesday for £2,200 in 1931 and played in four matches of that year's FA Cup run, including the final. Gregg appeared to have given Blues an early lead at Wembley but his goal was ruled out for offside. Overall he scored 15 times for Blues in 75 appearances before joining Chelsea.

SATURDAY 4th FEBRUARY 2017

A late Lukas Jutkiewicz goal gave Blues manager Gianfranco Zola his first win in 11 attempts since taking charge of the team. Jutkiewicz struck in the 75th minute to give Birmingham a 1-0 win against Fulham at St Andrew's.

WEDNESDAY 5th FEBRUARY 1936

Blues goalkeeper Harry Hibbs won his final cap as England went down 2-1 to Wales in a Home Championship match at Molineux. It was Hibbs' 25th England cap, which was a record for a keeper at the time, and remains a record for a Blue with the national team.

WEDNESDAY 6th FEBRUARY 1957

Birmingham City defender Trevor Smith won his second England B cap as Scotland were beaten 4-1 in an international friendly at St Andrew's. Brian Pilkington, Brian Clough, Peter Thompson and Harry Hooper scored the England goals in front of a crowd of 39,736. Smith, who went on to win two full England caps, was a fixture at the heart of the Birmingham defence for over a decade after making his debut in 1953. He made 430 appearances for Blues, won a Second Division title, the League Cup and played in the finals of both the FA Cup and Inter-Cities Fairs Cup.

THURSDAY 6th FEBRUARY 1958

Eight Manchester United players died when their plane crashed whilst attempting to take-off in Munich on the return trip from a European Cup match in Belgrade. Amongst the survivors was former Blues right-wing Johnny Berry. Berry played 104 matches for Birmingham City between 1946 and 1951 and scored six goals before joining Manchester United. The injuries he sustained at Munich ended his football career at the age of just 31.

SATURDAY 7th FEBRUARY 1931

Blues legend Joe Bradford scored all four goals as Blackburn Rovers were beaten 4-1 at Ewood Park. It was the last of Bradford's club record 13 hat-tricks.

SUNDAY 7th FEBRUARY 2010

Blues boss Alex McLeish set a Premier League record when he named an unchanged starting line-up for the 12th match in succession. The team of Joe Hart, Stephen Carr, Liam Ridgewell, Roger Johnson, Scott Dann, Lee Bowyer, Seb Larsson, Barry Ferguson, James McFadden, Cameron Jerome and Christian Benitez had all been selected to face Fulham the previous November and kept their places for the run. The final match in the sequence saw Wolves beaten 2-1 with two late goals from substitute Kevin Phillips.

SUNDAY 8th FEBRUARY 1931

Johnny Schofield was born in Atherstone, Warwickshire. The goalkeeper made his Blues debut in 1952 and racked up 237 appearances for Blues over the next 14 years, after taking over from Gil Merrick in goal. Schofield won the Second Division title and League Cup with Birmingham as well as playing in two Inter-Cities Fairs Cup finals. A working miner he described himself as 'bloody lucky' to survive the Baddesley Colliery pit explosion in November 1957. A year later he finished a match against Manchester United despite suffering a fractured skull. Schofield joined Wrexham following the arrival of Jim Herriot at the club and was later appointed as player-manager of Atherstone Town.

SATURDAY 8th FEBRUARY 1947

The Lord Mayor of Birmingham was amongst a crowd of 50,000 at St Andrew's as Birmingham City demolished Manchester City in the fifth round of the FA Cup. The pitch had to be cleared of snow before kick off but Blues took no time to warm up with Harold Bodle giving them a 9th minute lead. Cyril Trigg scored twice in the second half to extend the home side's lead. Frank Mitchell converted a penalty following a handball and Jock Mulraney added a fifth goal late on. The result sent Blues through to a quarter-final clash at Anfield, which they lost 4-1.

FRIDAY 9th FEBRUARY 1979

Blues forward Trevor Francis became the first ever £1m player when he transferred to English champions Nottingham Forest. The fee agreed between the clubs was £975,000 but the final figure was £1.18m after VAT and levies were added. The deal comfortably smashed the previous British transfer record, which had been set a month earlier when West Bromwich Albion paid Middlesbrough £516,000 for David Mills. Three months later Francis scored the winning goal for Forest in the European Cup final against Malmo in Munich.

SATURDAY 9th FEBRUARY 1980

A nine-minute Keith Bertschin hat-trick destroyed Orient in a Second Division match at St Andrew's. The Blues striker scored the opening goal of the game as he reacted quickest to a loose ball in the box after half an hour of play. In the 38th minute Bertschin volleyed a second goal from Archie Gemmill's free kick and 60 seconds later he completed his treble with a close-range header. Joe Mayo pulled a goal back for Orient to make the final score 3-1. Bertschin top scored for Blues with 12 league goals during the 1979/80 campaign.

TUESDAY 10th FEBRUARY 1942

Colin Green was born in Brymbo, Wales. The full-back began his professional football career with Everton and moved to St Andrew's in 1962 for a transfer fee of £12,000. He played 271 times for Blues, including both legs of the 1963 League Cup final, and scored one goal.

SATURDAY 10th FEBRUARY 1962

Striker Jimmy Harris could have had a hat-trick against Arsenal but had to settle for a solitary goal. Harris had already given Blues an early lead when Arsenal keeper Jack Kelsey saved his penalty kick two minutes before half-time. After the break he did manage to beat Kelsey again only to see this effort ruled out by the referee. The goal Harris did score proved enough, as Blues ran out 1-0 winners over the Gunners. In four seasons with Blues between 1960 and 1964 Harris, who was a £20,000 signing from Everton, scored 53 goals in 115 appearances in all competitions.

WEDNESDAY 11th FEBRUARY 1920

Blues manager Frank Richards signed striker Joe Bradford from Peggs Green Victoria for an initial fee of £100, which rose to £125 once the player had made his debut. The fee proved to be money well spent as Bradford's goals helped fire the club's promotion campaign the following season. His total of 267 Birmingham City goals in all competitions remains a club record.

SATURDAY 11th FEBRUARY 1939

A record crowd of 67,341 crammed inside St Andrew's to see Blues take on league leaders Everton in a fifth-round FA Cup tie. The bumper attendance, which produced record receipts of £4,556, were treated to end-to-end football. Owen Madden gave Blues the lead a minute before the break with a deflected shot but Everton hit back within seconds through Irish international Alex Stevenson. Wally Boyes gave Everton the lead on the hour when his shot bounced in off Tommy Lawton. Then, with ten minutes left, Madden headed his second of the match to make it 2-2 and send the tie to a replay, which Everton won 2-1. The visitors went on to win the league title at the end of the season while Blues were relegated after 18 seasons of top-flight football.

SUNDAY 11th FEBRUARY 1996

Despite a battling performance, Birmingham City lost the first leg of their League Cup semi-final against Premier League Leeds United. Blues led through a Kevin Francis goal but were pegged back when former Leeds defender Chris Whyte put the ball into his own net. Ghanaian international Tony Yeboah struck to give Leeds the edge and the top-flight side showed their class in the second leg as they coasted to a 3-0 win.

TUESDAY 12th FEBRUARY 1963

Trevor Matthewson was born in Sheffield, South Yorkshire. The 6ft 4in centre-half arrived at St Andrew's from Lincoln City for £45,000 in August 1989 and played in every Blues league match for the next two seasons. He made 203 appearances for Birmingham, which included the 1991 Leyland-DAF Cup final, as well as helping win promotion the following year.

TUESDAY 13th FEBRUARY 1979

A Graeme Souness goal condemned Blues to a 1-0 defeat to Liverpool at Anfield. It was the team's eighth successive league defeat, equalling a club record.

SATURDAY 14th FEBRUARY 1931

Welsh international Ernie Curtis scored twice and Joe Bradford added a third as Birmingham City moved a step closer to Wembley with a comfortable 3-0 win over Watford.

THURSDAY 14th FEBRUARY 1974

Blues striker Bob Latchford was sold to Everton in a deal valued at £350,000 - a British transfer record. Birmingham received £80,000 in cash for Latchford with midfielder Howard Kendall and left-back Archie Styles arriving at St Andrew's as part of the deal. The Birmingham-born striker made his Blues debut in 1968 and scored 84 goals in 194 appearances for the club.

THURSDAY 14th FEBRUARY 2008

Len Boyd died in Melton Mowbray, Leicestershire aged 84. The wing-half joined Blues from Plymouth Argyle in 1949 for a fee of £17,500. Although his first full season at St Andrew's ended in the disappointment of relegation Boyd was made captain for the following campaign by manager Bob Brocklebank. Under his captaincy Birmingham City won the Second Division title, reached the FA Cup Final and achieved their highest ever league placing of 6th. Boyd played 281 times for Blues, scoring 15 goals, before back problems forced his retirement from football.

SATURDAY 15th FEBRUARY 1890

Blues thrashed Darwen 6-2 in a Football Alliance match. Freddie Wheldon scored twice against the Lancashire side with Leslie Wilcox scoring on his debut while Caesar Jenkyns, Jack Hallam and Will Devey all scored.

SATURDAY 15th FEBRUARY 1908

Birmingham City made it 11 games without defeat as Chelsea were held to a 2-2 draw at Stamford Bridge. Billy Jones and Edmund Eyre scored the Blues goals but the unbeaten streak was to no avail as the team headed for relegation.

SATURDAY 16th FEBRUARY 1946

A crowd of 56,615 were at St Andrew's to see Birmingham City beat Charlton Athletic 1-0 in a Football League South fixture. It was the largest home attendance during wartime football. Wilson Jones scored the winning goal for Blues with Charlton keeper Sam Bartram spurning a chance to level for the Addicks when he smashed a penalty against the crossbar.

SUNDAY 16th FEBRUARY 1986

Blues travelled to Coventry City and drew 4-4 with the Sky Blues in the club's first ever competitive Sunday fixture. A crowd of 14,271 at Highfield Road were treated to eight goals in a seesaw battle on the Sabbath. Andy Kennedy scored after just two minutes to give Blues the lead and Steve Whitton made it 2-0 to the visitors, who might have had more before the break but were twice denied by the woodwork. Dave Bennett scored early in the second half to give the home side hope and then won a penalty, which Brian Kilcline converted to level the scores. Midfielder Martin Kuhl slammed the ball into the roof of the net to restore the Blues lead only to see Bennett level the scores with a 20-yard drive. It looked like the visitors might snatch victory when Andy Kennedy scored his second of the match in the 83rd minute. But five minutes later Nick Pickering won Coventry's second penalty of the match and Kilcline once again successfully dispatched it.

SATURDAY 17th FEBRUARY 1923

A 7-1 thrashing at the hands of Sheffield United condemned Blues to an eighth consecutive league defeat, an unwanted club record that has since been equalled twice, in 1979 and again in 1985. United's Harry Johnson was Blues' main tormentor at Bramall Lane with four goals while Albert Rawson, making his Birmingham debut after joining from the Blades just three days earlier, scored the visitors' consolation goal.

THURSDAY 17th FEBRUARY 1994

Birmingham City were hit with a record £55,000 fine by the Football League for illegally approaching manager Barry Fry who had quit his post at Southend United and joined Blues the previous December.

TUESDAY 17th FEBRUARY 2015

Birmingham City owners Birmingham International Holdings Limited (BIHL) confirmed it had appointed voluntary receivers from international accounting firm Ernst & Young. In a statement the club said it, 'wishes to reassure its supporters and staff most emphatically that no winding up petition has been filed against BIHL and that it is therefore not in liquidation'.

SATURDAY 18th FEBRUARY 1956

A late Peter Murphy goal at The Hawthorns continued Blues' away day success in the FA Cup. The 1-0 victory over West Bromwich Albion was the third victory on the road as Birmingham City headed for Wembley.

SATURDAY 18th FEBRUARY 2012

Eventual FA Cup winners Chelsea were given a fright at Stamford Bridge when David Murphy gave Blues an early lead. Colin Doyle saved Juan Mata's penalty kick as City enjoyed the better of the first half. However, Daniel Sturridge's second-half header made it 1-1 and sent the tie back to St Andrew's.

SATURDAY 19th FEBRUARY 1955

Eddie Brown scored direct from a corner kick as Blues edged past Doncaster Rovers in the FA Cup. Brown opened the scoring in this fifth round tie straight from the set piece and added a second on 53 minutes after Rovers had briefly levelled the scores.

SATURDAY 20th FEBRUARY 1971

Boy wonder Trevor Francis scored all four goals as Blues comprehensively beat Bolton Wanderers in a Second Division clash at St Andrew's. Francis put Blues ahead in the 16th minute, flicking the ball over the head of Bolton keeper Alan Boswell before heading home. He volleyed a second two minutes later and completed his hat-trick in the 78th minute slotting home the rebound after Phil Summerill's shot was parried. Francis was injured bravely heading in his fourth five minutes later and left the pitch to a standing ovation. The 16-year-old remains the youngest player to score a league hat-trick in England, a feat that led to Bolton's Nat Lofthouse labelling Francis 'an astonishing player'.

SUNDAY 21st FEBRUARY 1999

St Andrew's became an all-seater stadium as the Railway Stand was officially opened for a 0-0 draw with Bolton Wanderers. The two-tier stand can hold up to 8,000 fans and has since been renamed in honour of the club's legendary goalkeeper Gil Merrick, who made a record 551 appearances for Blues.

SUNDAY 22nd FEBRUARY 1998

Blues defender Michael Johnson finally broke his goal drought with his first career goal, in his 250th professional appearance, as he sealed victory against Sheffield United. Johnson's second-half strike put Birmingham 2-0 up against the Blades after Martin Grainger had opened the scoring from 25 yards.

SUNDAY 22nd FEBRUARY 2004

Stern John's dramatic 94th minute strike capped a late comeback and earned Blues a point at Villa Park. Villa had gone into the derby match in great form and were looking for a fifth successive win. It looked as if they might get it as they went two up through Darius Vassell and Thomas Hitzlsperger. But Blues were in no mood to roll over and pulled a goal back when Mikael Forssell side footed home from Clinton Morrison's lay off. Then with time running out John pounced on a rebound to level from close range.

MONDAY 23rd FEBRUARY 1903

A rearranged fixture saw Small Heath comprehensively beaten 4-0 at Manchester City. The result was a hard one for Blues to swallow as they had been leading the original match 1-0 with just seven minutes left on the clock when fog caused the referee to abandon the game.

SATURDAY 24th FEBRUARY 1940

Blues fell to their worst defeat of World War Two football as they were hit for six by West Bromwich Albion. Welsh international George Edwards scored City's consolation goal. Edwards was stationed in the Midlands while serving with the RAF and guested for both Blues and Coventry City. He turned professional with Birmingham in 1944 and scored nine goals in 99 appearances.

SATURDAY 24th FEBRUARY 1951

James Higgins scored after just 20 seconds to give Blues a decisive advantage in an FA Cup quarter-final tie at St Andrew's. One goal proved to be enough to knock Manchester United out of the competition in front of 50,000 fans.

SATURDAY 25th FEBRUARY 1893

Small Heath goalkeeper Chris Charsley became the first player from the club to win an England cap when he played against Ireland in a Home Championship match at Wellington Road in Birmingham. England won the match by a convincing 6-1 scoreline with the Reverend Walter Gilliat scoring a hat-trick. It was Charsley's only cap for his country.

WEDNESDAY 25th FEBRUARY 1925

Arthur Atkins was born in Tokyo, Japan. Although born in the Far East, the centre-half was educated in Erdington where he came to the attention of Birmingham City. After signing professional forms in 1948 he made his Blues debut 12 months later. Atkins was a key member of the side that got to the FA Cup semi-finals in 1951. Over five seasons the defender made 105 City appearances without scoring before moving to Shrewsbury Town.

SATURDAY 25th FEBRUARY 1978

Trevor Francis scored the only goal of the game as Aston Villa were beaten in the Second City derby at St Andrew's. The 1-0 Blues victory secured a second successive league double over Villa and a fifth successive win in the derby, the club's best run to date.

SUNDAY 25th FEBRUARY 2001

Blues lost the League Cup final to Liverpool in heartbreaking fashion. Misses from Martin Grainger and Andrew Johnson ensured City's barren run in penalty shoot-outs continued and gave Liverpool their sixth victory in the competition. Birmingham had trailed for almost an hour to Robbie Fowler's strike but in the final minute Stephane Henchoz upended Martin O'Connor and Darren Purse converted the spot kick. A goalless extra-time period saw a major English final go to a penalty shoot-out for the first time.

THURSDAY 26th FEBRUARY 1891

Small Heath beat Nottingham Forest, the leaders of the Football Alliance, in a nine-goal thriller at the Town Ground. Welsh centre-half Caesar Jenkyns scored twice while captain and top scorer Will Devey, Tommy Hands and Charlie Short all got a goal apiece.

SATURDAY 27th FEBRUARY 1892

Small Heath centre-half Caesar Jenkyns became the first Blue to gain international recognition when he was selected to play for Wales in a Home Championship clash against Ireland. The match at Penrhyn Park, Bangor finished 1-1 with Benjamin Lewis scoring for the home side and Olphie Stanfield levelling for Ireland. In total, Jenkyns would win eight caps and score one international goal.

SUNDAY 27th FEBRUARY 2011

Birmingham City sprang a major shock to beat hot favourites Arsenal 2-1 and win the League Cup for the second time in the club's history. It was Blues' first appearance at Wembley since the 1956 FA Cup Final and their first since the stadium had been rebuilt. As expected Arsenal dominated the match, which was played in front of 88,851 fans, and rained in 20 shots on the Birmingham goal. However, the Gunners found Ben Foster in superb form in the Blues goal and a string of saves earned him the Man of the Match award - Foster became the first man to win the award twice following his performance for Manchester United in the 2009 final. Alex McLeish's team were unlucky not to get off to a dream start when Arsenal keeper Wojceich Szczesny fouled Lee Bowyer in the penalty area only to see the spot kick and red card ruled out by an errant offside flag. Birmingham took the lead in the 28th minute when Nikola Zigic flicked Roger Johnson's header past Szczesny. Robin van Persie levelled the scores 11 minutes later volleying in from Andrei Arshavin's cross. In the second half City managed to repel Arsenal's attacks and even hit the post through Keith Fahey. Then, with just six minutes left on the clock, a mix-up in the Arsenal defence between Szczesny and Laurent Koscielny allowed Oberfemi Martins to steal in and roll the ball into an unguarded net to recapture the League Cup for the first time since 1963.

WEDNESDAY 28th FEBRUARY 1906

Muntz Street hosted a record crowd of 34,000 spectators who watched Blues dispose of Tottenham Hotspur 2-0 in a FA Cup third round replay. Blues progressed thanks to goals from Benny Green and Arthur Mounteney.

MONDAY 28th FEBRUARY 1910

Only 1,000 were at St Andrew's to see Birmingham City beat Burnley 2-1 in a Second Division match. Fred Chapple and Walter Freeman scored Blues' goals in front of the equal-lowest crowd to watch a league game at the ground.

SUNDAY 28th FEBRUARY 1926

Eddie Brown was born in Preston, Lancashire. The centre forward almost went into the priesthood but instead turned professional with his hometown club. He joined Birmingham City in 1954 following an impressive spell with Coventry City. Brown was a key member of Blues' successful mid-1950s side. He scored 90 goals in 185 appearances for Blues in all competitions before moving to Leyton Orient in 1958.

TUESDAY 28th FEBRUARY 1967

The film *Privilege*, starring singer Paul Jones and model Jean Shrimpton, was released in the UK. The film's plot centred around the conversion of a pop singer into a messianic cult leader. It was shot on location in Birmingham with many of the crowd scenes filmed at St Andrew's.

FRIDAY 29th FEBRUARY 1980

Blues keeper Jeff Wealands saved a penalty to set up a 1-0 victory over Swansea City at the Vetch Field. Wealands denied Tommy Craig in the 40th minute and ten minutes after the restart Steve Lynex struck to give Blues a 1-0 win.

THURSDAY 29th FEBRUARY 1996

Birmingham City striker Steve Claridge was sold to Leicester City for £1.2m. Claridge had joined Blues two years earlier and the following season became the first Birmingham player to score 20 goals in a league campaign since Trevor Francis in 1977.

BIRMINGHAM CITY
On This Day

MARCH

SATURDAY 1st MARCH 1986

Birmingham City's terrible run of home form came to an end as a Wayne Clarke penalty and Robert Hopkins strike saw off Queens Park Rangers in the First Division. City had gone 12 matches since their last win at St Andrew's, which came against Leicester City the previous September.

SATURDAY 1st MARCH 2008

Finnish striker Mikael Forssell scored a 'perfect' hat-trick as Tottenham Hotspur were comfortably beaten 4-1 at St Andrew's. Forssell got a goal with each foot and a header. Seb Larsson curled a free kick past Spurs keeper Paul Robinson for the home side's other goal. Forssell ended the season with nine goals in the Premier League, which made him Birmingham City's top scorer for a third time.

SATURDAY 2nd MARCH 1901

Scottish centre forward Bob McRoberts hit five as Blackpool were thrashed 10-1 at Muntz Street. Fellow Scot Johnny McMillan scored twice while Arthur Archer and Jack Aston chipped in with a goal each as Blues headed for promotion.

SATURDAY 2nd MARCH 1963

A 2-1 defeat to Manchester City was Blues' first taste of action in ten weeks due to the 'Big Freeze of 1963', which caused multiple league and cup postponements. The team's previous game had been at Leyton Orient on 22nd December 1962. Stan Harris got Blues' goal as they went down at Maine Road.

WEDNESDAY 3rd MARCH 1920

Birmingham City smashed the club transfer record when they signed striker Joe Lane from Blackpool for £3,600. He had attracted Blues' attention with a remarkable scoring record of 65 league goals for the Tangerines in just 94 appearances, despite the interruption of World War One. Lane served in Egypt with the Hertfordshire Yeomanry during the war before resuming his football career in Lancashire. At St Andrew's he formed a deadly partnership with Harry Hampton and the duo contributed 31 goals to the 1920/21 promotion campaign. In total, he made 67 Blues appearances in all competitions scoring 26 times.

SATURDAY 3rd MARCH 1956

Birmingham City recorded another away day victory to stay on the road to Wembley. Arsenal were beaten 3-1 in front of 67,872 at Highbury with Peter Murphy maintaining his record of scoring in every round of the competition. Murphy smashed home Blues' second goal after a Gordon Astall header had given them an early lead. Eddie Brown put Blues three up after a fine Murphy solo run.

MONDAY 3rd MARCH 2003

Blues completed a first Premier League double over rivals Aston Villa with a 2-0 victory at Villa Park. A feisty Second City derby saw Villa finish the match with only nine men while Blues striker Geoff Horsfield ended the match in goal after an injury to Nico Vaesen. Villa's Dion Dublin saw red for head-butting Robbie Savage and Joey Gudjonsson followed for a two-footed tackle on Matthew Upson. Stan Lazaridis gave Blues the lead from a Jeff Kenna cross and Horsfield added a second after taking advantage of Villa keeper Peter Enckelman's indecision.

SATURDAY 4th MARCH 1905

Billy Jones scored twice, including one from the penalty spot, as Small Heath won 4-1 against Blackburn Rovers. Oakey Field and Billy Beer got Blues' other goals as the club headed for a 7th place finish in the First Division, which would remain its highest until the mid-1950s.

WEDNESDAY 4th MARCH 1931

A bumper crowd of 74,365 was at Stamford Bridge to see Chelsea host Birmingham City in a FA Cup quarter-final replay. The gate was a record for the London ground and the largest Blues had played in front of at the time. The two sides had drawn the original match 2-2 at St Andrew's, but Chelsea were hit by injuries and Blues took full advantage. George Briggs had a hand in all the goals with Jack Firth scoring once and Joe Bradford twice in a comfortable 3-0 win on their way to Wembley. Firth's strike was the only time a player other than Bradford or Ernie Curtis scored in the FA Cup run of 1931.

SATURDAY 4th MARCH 1972

Half-time substitute Mike O'Grady became the first loan player ever used by Blues when he was brought on during a 4-0 thumping of Norwich City. Bob Hatton scored twice while Bob Latchford and Roger Hynd got a goal apiece against the Canaries.

FRIDAY 5th MARCH 1993

After five months in the hands of the receivers Birmingham City FC was sold to David Sullivan and the Gold brothers, Ralph and David, for £700,000. Sullivan appointed Karren Brady as the club's managing director and promised to make a transfer kitty of £500,000 available.

SATURDAY 6th MARCH 1886

Small Heath Alliance's first extended FA Cup run came to a shuddering halt in the semi-finals as the team were comprehensively outplayed by West Bromwich Albion. It was the first time the club had reached the semi-final stage but they went down 4-0 at Aston Lower Grounds. Blues have reached the final four on eight further occasions.

SATURDAY 6th MARCH 1971

Phil Summerill scored after just 12 seconds to give Blues the lead against Watford at St Andrew's. The goal is the fastest in Birmingham history and set City on course for a comfortable 2-0 victory over the Hornets with Trevor Francis adding the second goal.

TUESDAY 7th MARCH 1922

Peter Murphy was born in West Hartlepool, County Durham. The inside-left began his football career with Coventry City before moving to London and winning a Championship medal with Arthur Rowe's 1951 Tottenham Hotspur side. The following year he dropped down a division to join Blues in a £20,000 deal. He scored a hat-trick on his Blues debut and was top scorer with 24 goals the following season. Murphy was Birmingham's top scorer in two further seasons as he helped the club to promotion in 1955 and a 6th place finish in the top flight the following year. He was also a member of the 1956 FA Cup Final side and was involved in the incident where Manchester City goalkeeper Bert Trautmann broke his neck. During his eight years at St Andrew's Murphy scored 127 goals in 278 appearances.

SATURDAY 8th MARCH 1890

Records were set as Nottingham Forest were thrashed 12-0 in a Football Alliance match at Muntz Street. The 12-goal winning margin is a club record that has since been equalled, but never bettered, while Will Devey's six goals remains a club record for a single match. Devey also became the first Small Heath player to score a hat-trick, although he was soon joined by George Short who also got three in the rout while Devey's brother Ted scored twice and Jack Hallam added another.

WEDNESDAY 8th MARCH 1933

Joe Bradford scored his eighth, and final goal, against Aston Villa as Blues took the spoils with a 3-2 win in the Second City derby. Bradford remains City's leading goal scorer against Villa with his total of eight. Tom Grovesnor and George Briggs scored Blues' other goals as City took revenge for a loss at Villa Park earlier in the season.

SATURDAY 9th MARCH 2002

Blues overcame both high winds and a two-goal deficit to claim a point in the West Midlands derby against promotion-chasing Wolverhampton Wanderers. The visitors took the lead through two headers from Paul Butler and Joleon Lescott, which were both teed up by Mark Kennedy's crosses. The winds damaged the roof of the Main Stand at St Andrew's but there was no lasting harm to Blues' play-off push after a stirring fight back. Stern John pounced on a Kevin Muscat mistake to pull a goal back and Paul Devlin scored on the stroke of half-time to level the scores. Blues had the better of the second half, with John missing three good chances, but they could not take advantage.

FRIDAY 9th MARCH 2012

Kevan Broadhurst, Joe Gallagher, Alex Govan, Robert Hopkins, Roger Hynd, Malcolm Page and Garry Pendrey were inducted into the club's Hall of Fame. The players were honoured in an event staged by the Former Players' Association in the Legends' Lounge at St Andrew's. The players were voted into the Hall of Fame by a poll of City fans.

WEDNESDAY 10th MARCH 1920

Recent signings Harry Hampton and Joe Lane contributed six goals between them on their home debuts as Blues swept Nottingham Forest aside 8-0. Lane was the club's new record signing, costing £6,500 from Blackpool, while Hampton had moved across the city from local rivals Aston Villa. Hampton's haul of four goals took his tally to eight in just four matches since he arrived. Lane scored twice against Forest as did outside-right Lawrie Burkinshaw.

SATURDAY 10th MARCH 1951

The FA Cup semi-final between Blues and Blackpool attracted a crowd of 71,890 to Maine Road but ended goalless. The Tangerines, who had Stanley Matthews on the wing, were the favourites. City right-back Jack Badham switched flanks to mark Matthews and succeeded in keeping him contained while Blues came closest to scoring as Jackie Stewart rattled the woodwork in the final minute. The two sides met again in a replay at Goodison Park, which Blues lost 2-1.

TUESDAY 11th MARCH 1980

Blues enjoyed two slices of luck to help them into an early lead against Chelsea but took full advantage to run out 5-1 winners. Kevan Broadhurst's second-minute strike found the net courtesy of a huge deflection and Blues doubled their lead when a goalmouth scramble ended with Chelsea keeper Petar Borota punching the ball into his own net under pressure from Keith Bertschin. Chelsea did pull a goal back through Tommy Langley but found Blues in irresistible form. Two second-half goals from Alan Ainscow and a late Kevin Dillon strike sent City back to the top of the Second Division table.

SUNDAY 12th MARCH 1978

Jim Smith was appointed Blues manager following Sir Alf Ramsey's brief reign in charge. Smith, who was known as the 'Bald Eagle', presided over a rollercoaster four years at the club. He was unable to save the side from relegation in 1977/78 but led them back to the First Division at the first attempt. However, a mid-table finish in Blues' first season back in the top flight proved difficult to follow, and he was sacked in February 1982 to make way for Ron Saunders.

SATURDAY 13th MARCH 1937

Welsh international Seymour Morris got Blues off to a flying start with a goal after just 45 seconds against Brentford. A second goal for Morris, who would end the season as top scorer with 16, as well as strikes from Frank White and Fred Harris wrapped up a comfortable 4-0 win against the Bees.

SATURDAY 13th MARCH 1999

Blues' biggest crowd for five years were treated to a 4-0 beating of West Bromwich Albion in a West Midlands derby. There were 29,060 at St Andrew's to see top scorer Dele Adebola and Zimbabwe winger Peter Ndlovu combine to torment the Baggies. Adebola scored twice, sandwiching an Ndlovu effort, and Martin Grainger completed the win with a late tap-in.

SATURDAY 14th MARCH 1925

Bobby Brennan was born in Belfast, Northern Ireland. The forward became Blues' first £20,000 transfer when he arrived from Luton Town in the summer of 1949. He scored seven goals in 39 league appearances the following season, which saw City relegated from the First Division.

SATURDAY 14th MARCH 1931

Birmingham City reached the FA Cup Final for the first time in their history after beating Sunderland 2-0 in front of 43,570 at Elland Road. Welsh striker Ernie Curtis was the Blues hero with a goal in each half to book a place in the final. Curtis opened the scoring with a shot that cannoned in off the post after half an hour. Sunderland inside-right 'Hookey' Leonard had four good opportunities to level the scores but was denied by an inspired Harry Hibbs in Blues' goal. Finally, with three minutes left on the clock, Robert Middleton in the Sunderland goal saved Curtis' initial shot but the Welshman reacted fastest to slam the ball home.

WEDNESDAY 14th MARCH 1951

Goals from England internationals Stan Mortensen and Billy Perry put Blackpool through to the FA Cup Final at Birmingham's expense. The Tangerines won the semi-final replay at Goodison Park 2-1.

TUESDAY 15th MARCH 1887

Leslie Knighton was born in Church Gresley, Derbyshire. After his own playing career was cut short by injury Knighton turned to management. He arrived at St Andrew's in 1928 following spells at Huddersfield Town, Manchester City, Arsenal and Bournemouth. He led the team to the 1931 FA Cup Final although the team's league form was indifferent with a succession of mid-table finishes. Knighton left Blues in 1933 to head back to London and take charge of Chelsea.

SATURDAY 15th MARCH 1986

Scottish centre forward Andy Kennedy scored his seventh and final league goal of the season as Blues went down 2-1 to Tottenham Hotspur. Goals were a problem all season for Birmingham, who only hit the target 20 times in the league, and Kennedy's total of seven was enough to make him top scorer for a team that was heading for the drop.

MONDAY 16th MARCH 1908

Jimmy Windridge, who enjoyed two spells with Blues, scored one of England's goals in a 7-1 thrashing of Wales. Windridge would go on to score in a record-equalling six consecutive England matches.

WEDNESDAY 16th MARCH 1955

Birmingham City kept their promotion bid on track with a 4-1 win over Doncaster Rovers. Two goals in the opening eight minutes set Blues on course for a comprehensive win. Rovers goalkeeper Ken Hardwick failed to hold Roy Warhurst's shot in the 4th minute and Noel Kinsey found the top corner to double the lead four minutes later. Although Jimmy Walker pulled a goal back for the visitors Gordon Astall restored the two-goal cushion from the penalty spot following a handball. Straight from the kick-off Kinsey combined with Jackie Lane to tee up Peter Murphy for a fourth Blues goal.

SATURDAY 16th MARCH 1974

A lucky Joe Gallagher goal, the ball looping in off a tackle with only nine minutes left, gave Blues a 1-0 win over Manchester United at St Andrew's.

SATURDAY 17th MARCH 1894

Ardwick were thrashed 10-2 as Small Heath embarked on a six-match winning run that would earn them promotion to the First Division via a Test match. Frank Mobley led the demolition of the Manchester club with a hat-trick. Freddie Wheldon scored twice, as did Jack Hallam, while Caesar Jenkyns, Billy Walton and Tommy Hands got a goal each.

TUESDAY 17th MARCH 1981

Frank Worthington's 73rd-minute strike was the only goal of the game at St Andrew's as Blues beat Wolves 1-0 in a West Midlands derby.

SATURDAY 17th MARCH 2012

Former Blues midfielder Fabrice Muamba suffered a cardiac arrest while playing for Bolton Wanderers in an FA Cup quarter-final match against Tottenham Hotspur at White Hart Lane. The match was abandoned while Muamba received treatment on the pitch before being rushed to hospital. The player's heart stopped for 78 minutes and although he recovered the condition forced him to retire from professional football.

SATURDAY 18th MARCH 1972

A crowd of 52,470 were at St Andrew's to see Blues beat Huddersfield Town 3-1 in the FA Cup quarter-finals. Welsh international Malcolm Page gave Blues a first-half lead with his only goal of the season. After the break goals from Bob Latchford and Bob Hatton ensured Birmingham's safe passage to the semi-finals.

SATURDAY 18th MARCH 2000

On-loan striker Isaiah Rankin scored twice as Birmingham City brushed aside Barnsley 3-1 in this First Division clash. Defender David Holdsworth scored Blues' third goal and Rankin almost had a hat-trick but saw his shot cannon off the bar. The striker played 13 matches for City in a loan spell from Bradford City and scored four times.

SATURDAY 19th MARCH 1904

Goals from Billy Beer, Freddie Wilcox and Benny Green helped Blues record a convincing 3-0 win over West Midlands rivals Wolverhampton Wanderers at Muntz Street.

SATURDAY 20th MARCH 1971

Blues striker Phil Summerill scored twice to set up a 3-1 win over Sunderland in a Second Division fixture. Birmingham-born Summerill opened the scoring after just three minutes and doubled City's lead with a spot kick. Trevor Francis made it 3-0 before half-time with Dave Watson replying for the Black Cats. Summerill would finish as Blues' top scorer for the third season in succession with 21 goals.

SATURDAY 21st MARCH 1896

Dickie Dale was born in Willington, County Durham. The wing-half joined Blues in 1922 and made his debut the following season. Over the next five years he made 151 appearances in all competitions without ever scoring a goal.

TUESDAY 21st MARCH 1972

In-form strikers Bob Latchford and Bob Hatton scored a goal apiece as Blues were held 2-2 at Carlisle United. The two strikers combined for 49 goals during the 1971/72 season as Blues secured promotion back to the First Division.

TUESDAY 21st MARCH 2006

Blues fell to their worst ever FA Cup defeat as they were crushed 7-0 by Liverpool in the quarter-finals at St Andrew's. City fell behind after just 55 seconds when Sami Hyypia headed in from a Steven Gerrard free-kick. Soon afterwards Peter Crouch scored with a downward header and the Liverpool striker side-footed home the visitors' third just before the break. Fernando Morientes scored on the hour and John Arne Riise's drive made it 5-0. An Olivier Tebily's own goal and a Djibril Cisse shot completed the rout.

SATURDAY 22nd MARCH 1986

Birmingham's hopes of First Division survival were boosted by a 3-0 win over Aston Villa at Villa Park. Striker Wayne Clarke capitalised on two errors in the Villa defence to give Blues a comfortable lead at the break. Steve Whitton took advantage of further mistakes in the home rearguard to complete the win. The victory was City's last one of a season that was destined to end in relegation to the Second Division.

SATURDAY 23rd MARCH 1907

Sheffield Wednesday beat Arsenal 3-1 as St Andrew's hosted an FA Cup semi-final match for the first time. Wednesday would go on to lift the trophy after beating Everton 2-1 in the final at the Crystal Palace in London.

SATURDAY 23rd MARCH 1946

Inside-left Harold Bodle spurned a golden opportunity to send Blues to Wembley in the final minute of the FA Cup semi-final against Derby County at Hillsborough. A crowd of 65,013 were at the Sheffield ground to see Birmingham take on Derby. Jock Mulraney scored for Blues and the scores were locked at 1-1 with time running out when Bodle went clean through on the Derby goal but the chance went begging when he tamely shot straight at Rams goalkeeper Vic Woodley and the tie went to a replay.

SATURDAY 23rd MARCH 1957

Former Blue Johnny Berry opened the scoring for Manchester United in the FA Cup semi-final against Birmingham City at Hillsborough. Bobby Charlton added a second goal a minute later as the league champions ran out 2-0 winners. United would go on to retain their title but lose the FA Cup final to Aston Villa.

SATURDAY 24th MARCH 1894

Small Heath's rich goal-scoring form continued as a 6-0 thrashing of Burslem Port Vale made it 19 goals in a week. Blues had put 10 past Ardwick the previous Saturday and three past Rotherham Town just 24 hours earlier.

MONDAY 24th MARCH 2014

Bryan Orritt died in Johannesburg, South Africa, aged 77. The versatile Welshman who could play at wing-half, centre-forward or left-wing, made 119 appearances for Blues between 1956 and 1962 and scored 27 goals. Orritt featured in both of the club's Inter-Cities Fairs Cup final appearances as well as earning Wales Under-23 caps while at St Andrew's. He moved on to Middlesbrough, where he became the first substitute used by the club, before emigrating to South Africa in 1966.

SATURDAY 25th MARCH 1972

The winner of the *Sports Argus* competition to design a new Birmingham City crest was announced in the match programme for the 1-0 victory over Luton Town. Michael Wood, a conversion engineer with the West Midlands Gas Board from Burntwood in Staffordshire, won with his design of line-drawn globe and ball, with a ribbon carrying the club name and date of foundation, in plain blue and white. The programme said, 'Here it is the new Birmingham City club badge... It was picked out from the huge entry in a special competition. The players will wear it on their jerseys next season and will also be worn on club blazers and ties.' The badge was added onto the playing kit four years later.

SATURDAY 25th MARCH 1989

Birmingham City's visit to Filbert Street ended in a 2-0 loss to Leicester City that heralded a winless run of seven matches. Blues lost five of those matches as relegation to the Third Division beckoned for the first time in the club's history.

MONDAY 26th MARCH 1951

A 2-1 defeat to Cardiff City at Ninian Park would prove crucial to the outcome of the 1950/51 campaign. Blues travelled to the Welsh capital for a third match in four days having beaten Hull City on the previous Saturday and drawn with Cardiff at home 48 hours before that. Inside-forward Ken Rowley scored for Birmingham in Cardiff but could not prevent a 2-1 defeat and although Blues only lost once more during the season they were edged out of third place, and promotion, by Cardiff who finished a point ahead of them.

SATURDAY 26th MARCH 1983

A stunning Mick Ferguson volley put Birmingham City on track for a vital 3-0 win over Notts County as they battled against relegation. Ferguson doubled Blues' lead with a penalty and a second-half Mick Harford strike completed the victory. Ferguson, who was on loan from Everton at St Andrew's, finished the season as top scorer with eight goals as City finished safely above the drop zone.

SATURDAY 26th MARCH 1994

Andy Saville's 90th-minute strike finally ended Blues' winless run with victory over Middlesbrough. City had gone 14 league matches without a win before this First Division fixture. Manager Barry Fry gave a debut to wing Mark Ward and top-scorer Saville's late goal gave them a much-needed win.

WEDNESDAY 27th MARCH 1946

A record crowd of 80,407 were at Maine Road to see the FA Cup semi-final replay between Blues and Derby County. After a goalless 90 minutes the match turned in Derby's favour during extra time when City defender Ted Duckhouse suffered a broken leg leaving Blues with only ten men. Derby took full advantage scoring four times to book a place at Wembley where they went on to beat Charlton Athletic to win the first post-World War Two FA Cup.

WEDNESDAY 27th MARCH 1963

Blues took a slender advantage in the League Cup semi-final against Bury after winning the first leg 3-2 at St Andrew's. The victory could have been more emphatic but Bertie Auld missed a penalty and soon afterwards a lapse in defensive concentration allowed Bury to score their second goal of the night. The visitors had led 1-0 at half-time before conceding three goals in 18 minutes as Birmingham took control of the tie. Peter Bullock got City's equaliser with a clinical finish on 61 minutes, Auld converted a Jimmy Bloomfield cross for a second and Ken Leek headed in a third goal.

SATURDAY 27th MARCH 1971

Trevor Francis scored in an eighth consecutive league game for Blues as his third minute goal gave Birmingham the lead against Cardiff City. Phil Summerill scored a second goal after 75 minutes as Blues won 2-0 at St Andrew's.

SATURDAY 28th MARCH 1998

Defender Michael Johnson scored a last-minute winner to edge the West Midlands derby against West Bromwich Albion 1-0. It was Johnson's third goal in a month after he had waited eight years to score his first as a professional footballer.

FRIDAY 29th MARCH 1912

Wally Halsall was born in Liverpool, Merseyside. The centre-half was released by Blackburn Rovers in 1938 after the arrival of Birmingham City's Charlie Calladine at Ewood Park. Halsall was signed by Blues and played in 21 league fixtures of the 1938/39 campaign, which ended in relegation, before being sold to Chesterfield for £875.

TUESDAY 29th MARCH 1960

Reigning Inter-Cities Fairs Cup holders Barcelona, a team that boasted 'the greatest collection of international stars by any European club' according to one national newspaper, visited St Andrew's for the first leg of the 1960 final. The illustrious visitors were held to a 0-0 draw during a torrential downpour in Birmingham. The wet weather did not put off a crowd of 40,524 from attending and they saw the home side create the better chances with Harry Hooper and Don Weston both denied by last-ditch Barca defending.

SATURDAY 29th MARCH 1997

A colour clash between Birmingham's away kit and Crystal Palace's home strip caused Blues to take the field in a borrowed Eagles kit at Selhurst Park. The visitors overcame both the unfamiliar colour scheme and the sending off of Martyn O'Connor to win 1-0 thanks to a Martin Grainger goal. The match was the second in a 10-game unbeaten run that ended Trevor Francis' first full season in charge of Birmingham.

SATURDAY 30th MARCH 1895

Welsh international centre-half Caesar Jenkyns was sent off for the second time in his Small Heath career as a heavy defeat at Derby County ended in a fight on the pitch. Small Heath lost 4-1 with Jenkyns involved in unsavoury scenes with spectators and he never played for the Small Heath again.

SATURDAY 30th MARCH 1968

A crowd of 51,576 watched as Birmingham City took on Chelsea in the FA Cup quarter-finals at St Andrew's. A solitary Fred Pickering goal decided the match 1-0 in Blues' favour and set up a semi-final date with West Bromwich Albion.

WEDNESDAY 30th MARCH 1977

Birmingham City legend Trevor Francis opened his international goal-scoring account with a strike in his second outing for England. Francis scored in a comprehensive 5-0 win over Luxembourg in a World Cup qualifier at Wembley. Mick Channon scored twice for England while Liverpool's Kevin Keegan and Ray Kennedy also found the back of the net. Francis won 11 caps and scored two goals whilst a Birmingham City player. Overall he played 52 times for his country and scored 12 goals, including two at the 1982 World Cup finals in Spain.

SATURDAY 31st MARCH 1894

The goals continued to flow for Small Heath as they moved closer to promotion with a 4-1 win over Woolwich Arsenal. Caesar Jenkyns, Freddie Wheldon, Frank Mobley and Jack Hallam scored a goal each as Blues reached a century of league goals for the season. Mobley and Wheldon accounted for 46 of those goals between them, with 24 and 22 respectively. It was the first time in Football League history that two players from one club had passed the 20-goal mark in the same season.

SATURDAY 31st MARCH 1984

Goals from Welsh international Byron Stevenson and Howard Gayle clinched a 2-1 victory in the Second City derby against Aston Villa. Unfortunately, the result was Blues' final win of a season that was destined to end in the drop to the Second Division. Gayle finished the season with eight league goals, equal with Mick Harford. The striker had joined Birmingham City from Liverpool, where he had been the first black player to represent the club, in 1983. Gayle scored 11 goals in 59 appearances for Blues before moving to Sunderland.

MONDAY 31st MARCH 1986

A 3-0 defeat to Brian Clough's Nottingham Forest side at the City Ground heralded a seven-game losing run that ended in the relegation trapdoor out of the First Division. Nigel Clough opened the scoring from the penalty spot with Dutch defender Johnny Metgod adding a second and Neil Webb completing the win with a late goal.

BIRMINGHAM CITY
On This Day

APRIL

SATURDAY 1st APRIL 1893

Small Heath's 3-2 win over Ardwick clinched the Second Division title. The victory also completed the club's first season in the Football League with an unbeaten home record. Two goals for outside-right Jack Hallam and one for inside-forward Billy Walton gave Blues victory, which made it nine wins from ten matches at Muntz Street during the campaign. Despite finishing top of the second tier Small Heath were not promoted after failing to beat Newton Heath in the Test matches.

SATURDAY 1st APRIL 1899

Inside-left Walter Abbott scored a hat-trick as Gainsborough Trinity were thrashed 6-1 at Muntz Street. The goals took Abbott's tally to 34 in the league, which made him the Second Division's top scorer for the season. Overall Abbott scored 42 goals during the campaign, which remains a club record. Also on target against Trinity were Walter Wigmore with two goals and Billy Bennett with one.

SATURDAY 1st APRIL 1978

Trevor Francis got the only goal of the game as Birmingham City triumphed 1-0 against Wolverhampton Wanderers at Molineux. Francis struck in the 33rd minute and the win was secured when Jim Montgomery saved a Steve Daly penalty shortly after the break.

SATURDAY 2nd APRIL 2005

Jermaine Pennant became the first professional footballer to play a first-team match while wearing an electronic tag. The winger was making his comeback following a 30-day spell in prison after being convicted of driving offences. Birmingham boss Steve Bruce said, 'Everyone's seen Jermaine playing with a tag, now let's let him get on with resurrecting his career.' On the pitch City drew 1-1 against Tottenham Hotspur with Darren Carter's equaliser earning Blues a point.

SATURDAY 3rd APRIL 1937

Welsh wing-half Dai Richards scored one of the longest goals in Blues history as he found the back of the net from 50 yards against Sheffield Wednesday. City's top scorer Seymour Morris added two more goals as Blues ran out convincing 3-0 winners at Hillsborough.

SATURDAY 3rd APRIL 1976

A 3-2 win over Aston Villa began a record run of five consecutive Second City derby wins for Birmingham City. Terry Hibbitt, Kenny Burns and Trevor Francis were all on target for Blues at St Andrew's.

SATURDAY 4th APRIL 1959

Birmingham City right-back Jeff Hall died from polio aged 29. The sudden death of Hall, who had played his last game for Blues just two weeks earlier, proved a wake-up call about the necessity for vaccinations in Britain. Demand for the Salk vaccine soared after Hall's widow Dawn spoke about the loss of her young, fit, international footballer husband on television. Emergency vaccination clinics had to be set up and supplies of the vaccine flown in from the United States to cope with the demand. Hall had made 227 appearances for Blues and scored one goal as well as winning 17 England caps. He was a member of City's 1955 Second Division title-winning team and played in the 1956 FA Cup Final.

SATURDAY 4th APRIL 1970

Centre-forward Bob Latchford and full-back Ray Martin were on target as Blues went down 4-2 to Hull City at St Andrew's. It was Martin's only goal for the club in 374 appearances, which were spread over 14 years with City. Martin won the club's Player of the Year award in the 1969/70 and 1970/71 seasons as well as serving as club captain and being awarded a testimonial match in 1971.

SATURDAY 5th APRIL 1958

Blues recorded their best away win of the 1957/58 season with a 6-1 thrashing of struggling Sunderland at Roker Park. City got off to a flying start and were four up within 14 minutes thanks to two goals from Bryan Orritt as well as one each from Harry Hooper and Peter Murphy. Gordon Astall added a fifth in the 54th minute before Don Revie, the future Leeds United and England manager, pulled one back for Sunderland. Eddie Brown, who had also hit the woodwork twice during the match, scored Birmingham's final goal when he fired home from a Hooper cross.

SATURDAY 5th APRIL 2008

Irish midfielder Damien Johnson was sent off for the fifth time in his Blues career as the team fell to a 2-0 defeat in a crunch relegation match at Wigan Athletic. Johnson was sent off for a lunge on Wigan's Kevin Kilbane shortly before half-time and holds the unwanted record for the most dismissals whilst representing Birmingham City. Johnson was a £100,000 signing from Blackburn Rovers in 2002, he played over 200 matches for Blues, and his red card total was one more than his goal tally of four.

SATURDAY 6th APRIL 1912

Blues debutant Arthur Reed scored twice as the Second Division leaders Burnley were shocked 4-0 in front of 35,000 at St Andrew's. Reed had already had one goal ruled out for offside by the time Jack Hall opened the scoring on 20 minutes. The new signing from Doncaster then added a second before half-time with a shot from the edge of the box. Walter Hastings slammed home from Dickie Gibson's cross to make it three before Reed helped himself to a second, as the division's top team were put to the sword in emphatic fashion by a rampant Blues side.

SATURDAY 7th APRIL 1894

Blues finished their Second Division campaign with a 3-0 victory over FA Cup winners Notts County. Two goals for Tommy Hands and one for Billy Walton made it 103 league goals for the season. More importantly the win clinched second place in the league above the Magpies and ensured they would face Darwen rather than Preston North End in the promotion/relegation Test matches.

SATURDAY 7th APRIL 1973

There were over 48,000 at St Andrew's to see Blues slow down Liverpool's title charge with a 2-1 win over the Reds. Bob Latchford and Bob Hatton scored a goal each with Tommy Smith pulling one back for the visitors. Liverpool's day got worse when Emlyn Hughes saw red in the final minute of the game, but Bill Shankly's men recovered to win the first league championship of his reign as manager at Anfield.

WEDNESDAY 8th APRIL 1908

Bob Brocklebank was born in Finchley, London. The inside-right scored over 100 goals for Burnley, most of them in the wartime leagues, before turning to management. He joined Birmingham City in February 1949 and although the side was relegated at the end of the season he did a fine job of rebuilding the team. Brocklebank signed a number of future Blues greats including Len Boyd, Alex Govan and Noel Kinsey. He led the side to the 1951 FA Cup semi-finals before resigning in 1954. Brocklebank left behind a team that won promotion six months later and enjoyed one of the club's most successful periods over the next few seasons.

MONDAY 8th APRIL 1963

Ken Leek's early strike gave Blues a crucial two-goal advantage in the second leg of the League Cup semi-final against Bury. The visitors held on despite Warren Bradley pulling a goal back, and crowd trouble that saw Blues keeper Johnny Schofield hit with a stone, to go through to the final courtesy of a 4-3 aggregate win.

MONDAY 8th APRIL 1985

A stuttering Blues side got their promotion bid back on track with a resounding bank holiday win over Sheffield United. Coming into this match Birmingham had only won one of their previous six games. However, a 4-1 win over the Blades started a run that would take them unbeaten to the end of the season and make them runners-up in the Second Division. Irish midfielder Gerry Daly gave Blues a first-half lead, which Andy Kennedy doubled two minutes after the restart. Top scorer Wayne Clarke also scored twice to take his tally to 18 for the season.

TUESDAY 8th APRIL 1969

Goalkeeper Dave Latchford made his Blues debut in a 2-1 win over Bury at Gigg Lane. Phil Summerill scored twice for Birmingham while Garry Pendrey's own goal pulled one back for the home side. Latchford would go on to make 269 appearances for Blues over the next 13 years, despite competing with the likes of Gary Sprake and Jim Montgomery for his place.

SATURDAY 9th APRIL 1966

Blues and Derby County shared ten goals in a crazy Second Division match at St Andrew's. Blues led three times but could not hold the visitors off and had to settle for a 5-5 draw. Birmingham midfielder Trevor Hockey opened the scoring after 15 minutes and although Blues were pegged back by Alan Durban's quick-fire double a Malcolm Beard penalty and Bobby Saxton's own goal put them back in control at half-time. After the break Ian Buxton briefly put Derby back on level terms before Beard's second goal and a Geoff Vowden header appeared to give Blues a decisive 5-3 lead. However, Derby hit back with time running out as Bobby Thomson put past Jim Herriot in the home goal and a minute later Durban completed his hat-trick.

WEDNESDAY 9th APRIL 1975

Blues crashed out of the FA Cup in heartbreaking fashion as Fulham's John Mitchell scored in the final minute of extra time of a semi-final replay. Mitchell also scored in the original tie at Hillsborough with Joe Gallagher levelling for Blues. The replay at Maine Road had appeared to be heading for penalties when Mitchell struck, sending the Cottagers to Wembley. It was the eighth time that Blues had played in the semi-finals of the FA Cup and it remains the last time they have reached the last four.

SATURDAY 10th APRIL 1926

Burnley forward Louis Page was Blues' tormentor-in-chief as the Clarets inflicted Birmingham's heaviest home defeat at the time. Page scored six goals as the visitors romped to a 7-1 win at St Andrew's. Joe Bradford scored Blues' consolation goal.

SATURDAY 10th APRIL 1948

The goal Birmingham City conceded in their 3-1 victory over Bradford Park Avenue was the last time their defence was breached during the 1947/48 campaign. Blues goalkeepers Gil Merrick and Jack Wheeler were beaten only 24 times during the season to set a club record that still stands today. The two Blues keepers kept a combined total of 20 clean sheets in 42 league matches.

GIL MERRICK

WEDNESDAY 11th APRIL 1866

Harry Morris was born in Birmingham. The right-half played for Small Heath in both the Football Alliance and the Football League. Later he would join the club's board and is credited with finding the site that would become St Andrew's. Morris played in the 1886 FA Cup semi-final against West Bromwich Albion and was present at Wembley 45 years later when Blues took on the same opposition.

SATURDAY 11th APRIL 1903

Needing a win to keep their promotion hopes alive Blues responded in emphatic fashion by thrashing Doncaster Rovers 12-0 to equal their biggest ever win. Small Heath led 3-0 at half-time before going on the rampage with nine goals in the second half. Bob McRoberts was involved in eight Blues goals, including scoring one, while Arthur Leonard and Freddie Wilcox scored four goals each in the rout. Charlie Field, Charlie Athersmith and Jack Dougherty completed Doncaster's miserable afternoon at Muntz Street.

MONDAY 12th APRIL 1993

Relegation-battling Blues blew a 4-1 lead at St Andrew's and went down 6-4 to Glenn Hoddle's Swindon Town. The home side had looked on course to secure a vital three points as goals from Dean Peer, John Frain, Paul Moulden and Andy Saville gave them a comfortable lead. Shaun Taylor's header had given Swindon a foothold in the game shortly before half-time but Saville's strike in the 51st minute appeared to have put the contest beyond the visitors. However, four goals in 18 minutes turned the match on its head as Swindon strikers Craig Maskell and Dave Mitchell scored twice each. Mitchell completed his hat-trick in the 89th minute to cap a remarkable comeback.

SATURDAY 13th APRIL 1895

Small Heath ensured their top-flight survival with a 2-0 victory over Sheffield United. Blues took the lead when an attempted clearance by United goalkeeper William 'Fatty' Foulkes rebounded off his team-mate Walter Hill for an own goal. Small Heath forward Frank Mobley made both the game and the club's First Division status safe with a second goal when he applied the finishing touch to Tommy Hands' break.

SATURDAY 13th APRIL 1940

Aston Villa provided the opposition for Harry Hibbs' testimonial match at St Andrew's. A crowd of 15,000 were in attendance and helped raise £650 for Blues and England goalkeeper. Hibbs was Birmingham City's first choice goalkeeper for 12 years racking up 388 appearances and playing in the 1931 FA Cup Final.

SATURDAY 13th APRIL 1946

Birmingham City wing-half Neil Dougall was part of the Scotland side that beat England 1-0 in a Victory International. Manchester United's Jimmy Delaney scored the only goal of the game at Hampden Park. Dougall made over 100 league and cup appearances for Blues, as well as being part of the side that won the 1946 Football League South wartime championship.

SATURDAY 14th APRIL 1945

The longest game in Blues history eventually ended after 153 minutes of football at Molineux. The regional wartime match against Wolverhampton Wanderers finished goalless after 90 minutes and the two managers agreed to play on until a goal was scored. Finally, at 5:45pm, Wolves and England defender Bill Morris broke the deadlock to claim victory.

SATURDAY 14th APRIL 2007

On-loan Arsenal striker Nicklas Bendtner scored a vital goal against Southampton to boost Blues' promotion hopes. Two losses over Easter had dented Birmingham's attempt to bounce straight back to the Premier League. A powerful Radhi Jaidi header gave City the lead against Saints and Bendtner doubled it late on after latching on to Andrew Cole's pass. The game finished 2-1 after Marek Saganowski pulled one back for the visitors. It was the first of four straight victories that secured promotion.

SATURDAY 15th APRIL 1939

A Wilson Jones goal gave Blues a 1-0 victory over Brentford at Griffin Park and sparked a late season rally. City won three of their last five games and drew the other two, but it was not enough to avoid the drop, and after spending most of the 1939/40 season in the bottom three they finished a point short of safety.

SATURDAY 15th APRIL 1972

A brave Blues performance could not prevent a 3-0 defeat to Don Revie's Leeds United in the FA Cup semi-final at Hillsborough. Goals in the opening 25 minutes from Mick Jones and Peter Lorimer put Leeds in control of the tie. Jones added a third after 65 minutes for the eventual Cup winners.

SATURDAY 16th APRIL 1977

Kenny Burns and Trevor Francis were both on target as Stoke City were beaten 2-0 at St Andrew's. It was Burns' 18th league goal of the season and he would finish with 20 in all competitions. Francis pipped him to top scorer with 21 goals, all of which came in the league.

MONDAY 17th APRIL 1933

Joe Bradford scored his 267th and final Blues goal as Sunderland were beaten 2-0 at St Andrew's. The striker's total remains the club record and he is the only player in Birmingham history to have scored over 150 goals for the team. Bradford scored 249 league goals and 18 in the FA Cup in 445 Blues appearances. He was top scorer, or joint-top scorer, for 11 consecutive seasons between 1922 and 1933 and also holds the club record for hat-tricks with 13.

WEDNESDAY 17th APRIL 1957

Blues topped Group B in the Inter-Cities Fairs Cup after completing the stage with a 2-1 win over Internazionale. Top scorer Alex Govan scored either side of the break at St Andrew's to complete the group stage unbeaten and set up a semi-final tie with Barcelona. Italian international striker Benito Lorenzi scored a late consolation for Inter.

TUESDAY 18th APRIL 1972

A 0-0 draw with Fulham at Craven Cottage was Blues' 17th draw of the season. One more draw and three wins would be enough for Freddie Goodwin's side to seal promotion back to the First Division after an absence of six years.

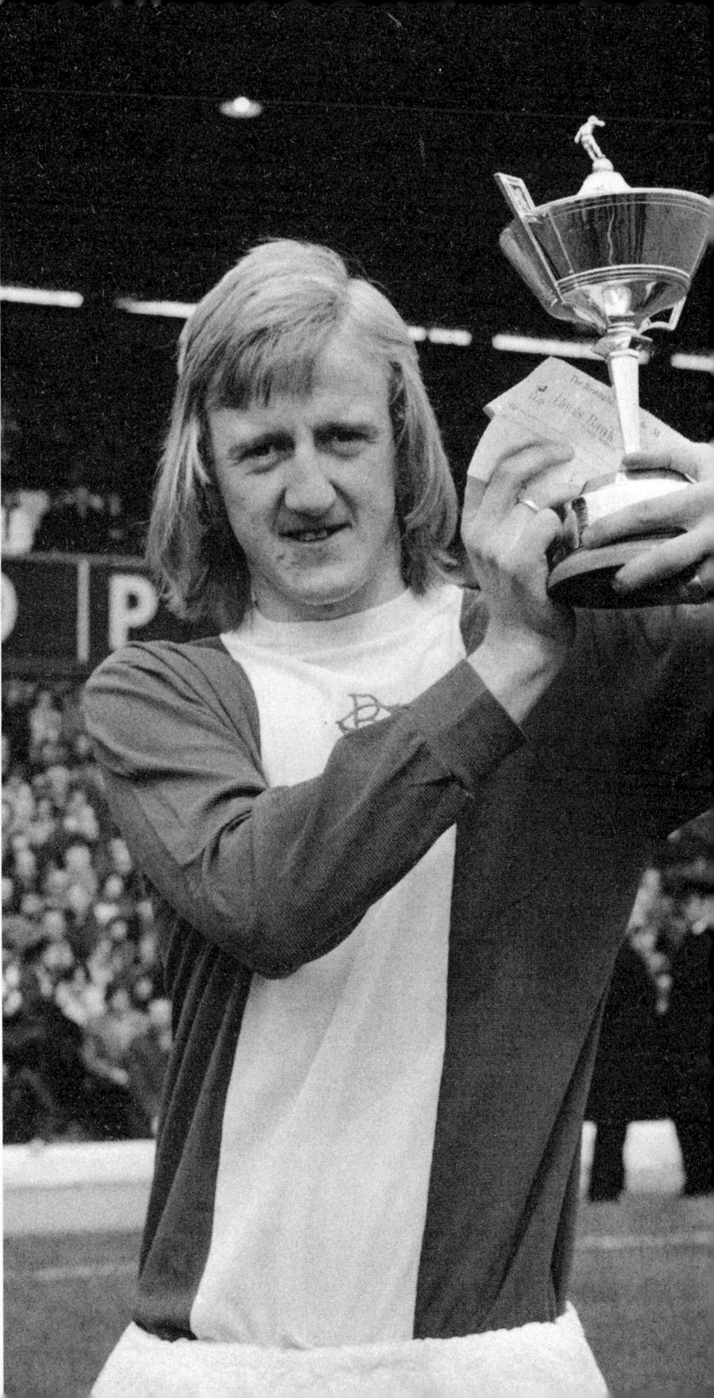

KENNY BURNS

SATURDAY 18th APRIL 1992

Birmingham City edged closer to promotion back to the Second Division with a 2-1 win over Hartlepool United. Trevor Matthewson and Nigel Gleghorn scored the goals as Terry Cooper's team moved to within one win of securing second place and a return to the second tier after two seasons in the Third Division.

WEDNESDAY 19th APRIL 1961

A 2-1 victory in the San Siro gave Birmingham the advantage at the end of the first leg of their Fairs Cup semi-final with Internazionale. Jimmy Harris gave Blues the lead in Milan and an own goal from Inter's Costanzo Balleri put them two up by the break. Italian international Eddie Firmani pulled one back for the hosts but Birmingham hung on to become the first English side to win at the San Siro, a feat not matched until Arsenal managed it 42 years later.

SATURDAY 19th APRIL 1980

A Keith Bertschin goal gave Blues a 1-0 victory over Luton Town at St Andrew's. The result began a run of two wins and two draws that would secure third place in the Second Division and a return to the top flight at the first attempt.

MONDAY 20th APRIL 1903

Small Heath confirmed promotion back to the First Division, and finished the season with a 100% home record, after beating Manchester United 2-1 at Muntz Street. Freddie Wilcox and Arthur Leonard scored the Blues goals as they won their 17th and final home game of the season. It was the third season in a row that Blues had changed division.

SATURDAY 20th APRIL 1957

Outside-left Alex Govan hit his fifth hat-trick of the season as Leeds United were thrashed 6-2 at St Andrew's. Eddie Brown scored twice while Gordon Astall was also on target against Leeds. Govan bagged four league trebles and another in the FA Cup during the 1956/57 season as he top scored for Blues with 30 goals in all competitions.

SATURDAY 21st APRIL 1956

A 5-2 victory over Bolton Wanderers ended a successful season for Blues who ended in their highest ever league position of 6th in the First Division. Wanderers gave Birmingham a helping hand on the day with two own goals scored by Johnny Wheeler and Malcolm Barras. Blues added three more goals through Noel Kinsey, Gordon Astall and Peter Warmington to complete their best top-flight campaign in style.

SATURDAY 22nd APRIL 1893

After finishing the season as the Second Division champions Small Heath met Newton Heath, who had finished bottom of the top flight, in a Test match to decide whether the two sides should swap divisions. Small Heath dominated the game, which was played at the Victoria Ground in Stoke, but could not make their superiority count. They fell behind to an Alf Farman goal against the run of play before Freddie Wheldon made it 1-1 and sent the tie to a replay.

WEDNESDAY 22nd APRIL 1964

Stan Lynn's 7th minute penalty put Blues on course for a 3-1 win over Liverpool. Ken Leek and Mike Hellawell scored further Birmingham goals before Roger Hunt got a late consolation for the Reds. Lynn's successful spot kick was the first of five he would convert in successive matches at the end of the 1963/64 season and the start of the following campaign.

MONDAY 23rd APRIL 1906

Former Wolverhampton Wanderers forward Jack Smith scored his one and only Blues goal as Blackburn Rovers were beaten 3-0. Arthur Mounteney and Benny Green scored Birmingham's other goals against Rovers. A win on the final day of the season against Manchester City would secure a second successive 7th place finish in the top flight.

SUNDAY 23rd APRIL 1995

Birmingham sub Paul Tait wrote himself into English football history and Blues' fans folklore after scoring the winning goal in the Auto-Windscreens Shields final. Normal time in the final had finished goalless against Tranmere Rovers and when Tait struck in the 103rd minute it was the first ever Wembley golden goal. Controversially, Tait then revealed a t-shirt taunting rivals Aston Villa, an action that cost him two weeks' wages.

SATURDAY 24th APRIL 1965

Wing-half Malcolm Beard scored his one and only Blues hat-trick in a 5-5 draw with Blackburn Rovers. Blues had already been relegated and only 8,887, the lowest attendance of the season, were at St Andrew's to see City and Rovers put on a ten-goal thriller. Birmingham manager Joe Mallett converted Beard to a striker for the afternoon and was rewarded with a treble as Blues twice came from two goals down to snatch a draw. Stan Lynn converted a penalty and Geoff Vowden was also on the score-sheet. At the other end debutant goalkeeper Billy Beel had to pick the ball out of his net five times, including after an own goal put past him by Terry Hennessey.

SATURDAY 25th APRIL 1931

Birmingham City faced West Bromwich Albion at Wembley Stadium having reached the FA Cup Final for the first time in the club's history. Blues were denied a dream start to the match when a linesman's flag ruled out Bob Gregg's sixth-minute header. City fell behind in the 24th minute when Ned Barkas' inadvertent touch gave Albion's William 'Ginger' Richardson a second chance to steer a loose ball into the net. Chances were missed at both ends before Joe Bradford equalised with a 25-yard shot in the 57th minute. Birmingham were only on level terms for one minute though before Richardson struck the winner from George Liddell's sliced clearance. The two goalkeepers, Blues' Harry Hibbs and the Baggies' Harold Pearson, were cousins.

TUESDAY 25th APRIL 1972

Over 40,000 were at St Andrew's to see Blues extend their unbeaten streak at home to 36 matches, which remains a club record. An Alan Campbell penalty and a second-half Trevor Francis strike sealed a 2-0 win over Hull City as promotion drew closer.

SATURDAY 25th APRIL 1992

Top scorer Nigel Gleghorn's 22nd goal of the season was enough to clinch automatic promotion from the Third Division with a 1-0 win over Shrewsbury Town. It was Blues' first win over bogey side Shrewsbury in 12 attempts and ensured promotion to the second tier.

THURSDAY 26th APRIL 1917

Benny Green was killed in action near Arras in France while serving as a Private with the King's Own (Royal Lancaster Regiment). The inside-forward was aged 34 at the time of his death. Prior to the war he had made 198 Blues appearances and scored 46 goals, including the first goal scored at St Andrew's.

THURSDAY 27th APRIL 1893

Small Heath and Newton Heath met at the Olive Grove in Sheffield in a replay of their promotion/relegation Test match. Billy Walton gave Blues the lead and Frank Mobley pegged the score back to 2-2 after Newton Heath had gone in front. However, the First Division side finished much stronger and three goals in the final 18 minutes made the final score 5-2 and condemned Small Heath to another season in the second tier.

MONDAY 27th APRIL 1896

Small Heath thrashed Manchester City 8-0 in their final promotion/relegation Test match after they had finished 15th in the First Division. Jack Jones and Freddie Wheldon both scored hat-tricks against the Citizens with Walter Abbott and Jack Hallam adding a goal each. The result proved too little, too late, as two losses and a draw in earlier Test matches had already sent Small Heath back down to the Second Division.

SATURDAY 27th APRIL 1968

Birmingham City's FA Cup run ended in the semi-finals as they went down 2-0 to West Bromwich Albion at Villa Park. England international Jeff Astle, who scored in every round of that year's cup competition, and West Brom legend Tony Brown got the goals for the Baggies who went on to beat Everton 1-0 in the final.

SATURDAY 28TH APRIL 1894

Blues secured First Division status for the first time as Darwen were beaten 3-1 in a Test match at the Victoria Ground. Birmingham had finished second in the Second Division table while their opponents had ended the season second bottom of the top flight to set up the promotion/relegation clash. Goals from Jack Hallam, Billy Walton and 'Diamond' Freddie Wheldon ensured that the two teams swapped places for the following season.

SATURDAY 28th APRIL 1906

A 3-2 victory over Manchester City clinched a 7th place finish in the First Division, which equalled Blues' best performance at the time. Strikes from Benny Green and Billy Jones as well as an own goal from City's John Edmondson edged the contest for the home side. Goalkeeper Nat Robinson played in every Blues match of the season, the fourth time he had achieved the feat.

SATURDAY 28th APRIL 1934

Relegation-threatened Blues went on a seven-goal rampage at Filbert Street to secure a vital win that confirmed their First Division place. Birmingham had to overcome atrocious weather as well as their hosts before running out 7-3 winners against Leicester City. Sid Moffatt opened the scoring after just four minutes before Dave Magnall, Freddie Roberts, a Foxes own goal and a Billy Guest hat-trick made it a magnificent seven for Blues.

TUESDAY 29th APRIL 1941

Barry Bridges was born in Horsford, Norfolk. The striker made a name for himself as part of Tommy Docherty's Chelsea side in the early 1960s, winning the League Cup and earning an England call up. Blues manager Stan Cullis broke the club transfer record when he brought Bridges to St Andrew's for £55,000 in May 1966. Bridges scored 46 goals in 104 matches during his two seasons with Birmingham, helping the club reach the semi-finals of the League Cup in 1967 and the FA Cup the following season.

SATURDAY 29th APRIL 1978

Ex-Blues striker Bob Latchford won £10,000 when he scored twice in Everton's 6-0 thrashing of Chelsea at Goodison Park. The prize money had been offered by the *Daily Express* to the first top-flight striker to score 30 goals in the 1977/78 season.

WEDNESDAY 30th APRIL 1930

Despite beating Stockport County 3-0 on the last day of the season Blues finished rock bottom of the Second Division and needed re-election to continue playing in the Football League the following season.

BIRMINGHAM CITY
On This Day

MAY

SATURDAY 1st MAY 1948

A goalless draw against Tottenham Hotspur was enough to clinch the Second Division title for the third time in the club's history. Blues finished the season with 59 points – a club record under the two-points-for-a-win system – and returned to the top flight for the first time since World War Two.

TUESDAY 1st MAY 1979

Blues' woes on their travels continued at Maine Road in a match notable for the brief appearance of Blues sub Malcolm Briggs. Briggs was brought on for Alan Buckley in the 88th minute for his only senior outing, making his two minutes on the pitch the shortest Birmingham City career on record. Steve Lynex got the visitors' goal as the Blues went down 3-1 in Manchester on their way to relegation. It was the club's 19th away defeat of the season, 18 of them consecutive, both unwanted records.

TUESDAY 2nd MAY 1972

Over 15,000 Birmingham City fans made the trip down to London to see Blues clinch promotion with a 1-0 win over Orient. Bob Latchford got the crucial goal, his 30th of the season, which edged out Millwall for second place in the Second Division table and sealed a return to the top flight after an absence of seven years. Latchford rose highest to head home Gordon Taylor's cross in the 58th minute.

THURSDAY 2nd MAY 2002

Stern John's last-minute winner sent Birmingham through to the play-off final in Cardiff in dramatic fashion. The Trinidad & Tobago international tapped the ball into an empty net from three yards to end the Blues' play-off jinx. City had suffered play-off heartache losing at the semi-final stage in the three previous seasons. The semi-final tie with Millwall was on a knife-edge after a 1-1 draw at St Andrew's in the first leg. John had missed several good chances to score during the game at the New Den. The striker made amends with his last-gasp winner to send Blues through. The goal sparked unsavoury scenes with the home fans rioting after the final whistle.

SATURDAY 3rd MAY 1924

Blues goalkeeper Dan Tremelling's late penalty save denied Len Davies from 12 yards and stopped Cardiff City from becoming Football League champions. The Bluebirds had arrived at St Andrew's needing a win to take the title, but were held to a 0-0 draw by Blues, which made Huddersfield Town the champions. If Cardiff had won the Championship it would have been the only time that the title had ever gone to a non-English club.

WEDNESDAY 3rd MAY 1961

Striker Jimmy Harris scored twice to put Blues into their second successive Inter-Cities Fairs Cup final. Harris struck in the fourth minute to give Birmingham, who were already leading Internazionale 2-1 from the first leg, a useful cushion. He extended the advantage further with a goal just after the hour and although Enea Masiero pulled one back four minutes later it proved too little, too late, for Inter.

SUNDAY 3rd MAY 2009

Birmingham City sealed an instant return to the Premier League with a 2-1 win at Reading. Keith Fahey opened the scoring for Blues with a low 25-yard shot and top scorer Kevin Phillips doubled the lead on the hour. Reading substitute Marek Matejovsky got a goal back for the hosts, which made it a nervous finish, but Blues held on to clinch automatic promotion.

SATURDAY 3rd MAY 2014

Scottish defender Paul Caddis wrote himself into Blues folklore with a 93rd-minute header that saved the club from dropping into League One. Birmingham had gone into the final round of matches a point behind Doncaster Rovers, but crucially boasting a superior goal difference. Things did not look good when Lee Chung-Yong and future Blue Lukas Jutkiewicz put the home side 2-0 up at the Macron Stadium. Nikola Zigic's goal gave Blues hope, as did news filtering through to fans that Doncaster were losing at champions Leicester City. In the third minute of extra time Tim Ream cleared Zigic's shot off the line and Caddis was on hand to head home from close range sparking wild celebrations amongst the 3,500 travelling Blues fans.

WEDNESDAY 4th MAY 1955

Blues clinched the Second Division title in style with a 5-1 thrashing of Doncaster Rovers at Belle Vue. Two Gordon Astall goals and one apiece from Eddie Brown, Peter Murphy and Alex Govan meant Birmingham squeezed past Luton Town. Blues took top spot with a superior goal average after both sides had finished on 54 points. Captain Len Boyd said, 'The ground was packed and alive with supporters wearing the colours of Birmingham City. We knew we would win – and so too did those fans – and our performance that day was quite brilliant.'

WEDNESDAY 4th MAY 1960

Blues visited Barcelona for the second leg of the 1960 Inter-Cities Fairs Cup final with the scores locked at 0-0 after the first tie. Unfortunately the hard work that had kept Barcelona goalless for 90 minutes at St Andrew's was undone after just three minutes at the Camp Nou, when Eulogio Martinez gave the home side the lead in front of 70,000 spectators. Barca added a second three minutes later through Zoltan Czibor and the Hungarian scored again shortly after the break. Lluis Coll scored Barca's fourth goal before Harry Hooper got a late consolation for Blues.

SATURDAY 5th MAY 1956

Birmingham City became the first team to play in an FA Cup Final without hosting a home fixture. Blues went into the final as favourites but failed to get to grips with Manchester City's tactics, particularly the deep-lying centre forward Don Revie. Joe Hayes opened the scoring for the Citizens after being put clear by Revie's back heel but Noel Kinsey levelled with a shot that cannoned in off the post. And Blues were unlucky not to lead at half-time after Eddie Brown twice saw goals chalked off for offside. Two Manchester goals in two minutes, scored by Hayes and Bobby Johnstone, proved decisive in a 3-1 defeat. However, the final is mainly remembered for the bravery of Manchester's goalkeeper Bert Trautmann. The former prisoner of war played the final 17 minutes of the match with a broken bone in his neck after hurling himself at Peter Murphy's feet to make a save.

SATURDAY 6th MAY 1950

Full-back Dennis Jennings set the record as the oldest player ever to represent Birmingham in a competitive fixture at the age of 39 years and 290 days when he was selected to face Wolves at Molineux. Blues had already been relegated and a demoralised side went down 6-1 with Cyril Trigg scoring a consolation goal for Blues.

WEDNESDAY 6th MAY 1959

A Bunny Larkin strike gave Blues a 1-0 advantage after the home leg of their quarter-final tie with the Zagreb XI in the Inter-Cities Fairs Cup.

SATURDAY 6th MAY 1995

Blues visited Huddersfield Town for their final match of the season with both the Second Division title and the only automatic promotion spot on the line. Draws with Brighton and Brentford on the run in had given the Bees a chance to snatch both from Blues. However, City conquered their nerves to get the better of the Terriers. Steve Claridge got the breakthrough for Blues in the 72nd minute and Paul Tait made the game safe with five minutes left as a 2-1 win clinched promotion. Tait's goal was Blues' 87th in the league and 144th in all competitions for the season, a club record.

SATURDAY 7th MAY 1921

A 2-0 victory over Port Vale clinched the Second Division title on goal average from Cardiff City. Goals from top scorer Harry Hampton and outside-left George Davies made it a total of 79 league goals at an average of 2.08, as opposed to Cardiff's 1.84. Winger Johnny Crosbie was ever-present in the title-winning side.

SUNDAY 7th MAY 2017

A Che Adams strike secured a vital 1-0 win at Bristol City and preserved Blues' Championship status. Harry Redknapp was parachuted in for the final three games of the campaign after Gianfranco Zola had resigned with the team in a precarious position. Redknapp was able to steer the club to safety with crucial wins over Huddersfield Town and the Robins.

SATURDAY 8th MAY 1993

Striker Paul Moulden's fifth and final Birmingham City goal proved to be a vital one, when it secured a 1-0 win over Charlton Athletic that kept Blues in the First Division. City went into the final day of the season still at risk of the drop but roared on by a crowd of 22,234 at St Andrew's they took a crucial three points, which kept them safe at the expense of Cambridge United.

WEDNESDAY 8th MAY 1996

Blues beat Aston Villa 2-0 in the Birmingham Senior Cup final despite being reduced to eight men by three red cards. John Cornforth, Ian Jones and Paul Peschisolido all received their marching orders while Villa's Ben Petty was also sent for an early bath. City made light of the numerical disadvantage to win the cup through goals by Ricky Otto and Jason Bowen.

WEDNESDAY 8th MAY 1996

Future Blue Bruno N'Gotty scored the only goal of the 1996 Cup Winners' Cup final. The French defender's 29th-minute free kick gave Paris Saint-Germain a 1-0 victory over Rapid Vienna in Brussels and clinched the club's only European silverware to date. A decade later N'Gotty arrived at St Andrew's on a free transfer and the defender helped the side to regain its Premier League status in his one season with Blues.

WEDNESDAY 9th MAY 2012

A stirring late comeback fell just short as Blues once again suffered play-off heartache, this time at the hands of Blackpool. The Tangerines led 1-0 from the first leg at Bloomfield Road and looked to have booked their place at Wembley as they led by two on the night and three overall. Stephen Dobbie had opened the scoring with a shot that squirmed under Colin Doyle and Matt Phillips scored shortly after half-time but City never gave up. Nikola Zigic gave them hope with a cool finish in the 64th minute and nine minutes later Curtis Davies powered home a header from Jordon Mutch's cross. City then laid siege to the visitors' goal but could not find an equaliser.

CURTIS DAVIES

TUESDAY 10th MAY 1977

Two late goals gave Blues victory in a bad-tempered Second City derby and completed the league double over Aston Villa. Trevor Francis' 80th minute penalty completed a comeback after John Deehan had given Villa the lead in front of 43,271 at St Andrew's. Terry Hibbitt had scored the equalising goal five minutes earlier and in between Blues' two goals Joe Gallagher had seen red. He joined Villa's Leighton Phillips, who had received his marching orders after 30 minutes.

SATURDAY 11th MAY 1985

Leeds United fans rioted at St Andrew's causing over 500 injuries, including 96 police officers, and the death of a 15-year-old boy when a wall collapsed. The violence took place on the same day as the Bradford City stadium fire, which prompted a judicial inquiry. Describing events at St Andrew's in his report Mr Justice Popplewell said it had 'more resembled the Battle of Agincourt than a football match.'

SUNDAY 11th MAY 2008

Needing a win to have any chance of Premier League survival Blues responded with a convincing 4-1 victory over Blackburn Rovers. David Murphy gave Blues a first-half lead and although Rovers levelled through Morten Gamst Pedersen, two Cameron Jerome goals and a late Fabrice Muamba strike sealed the points. The win proved to be too little too late as both Fulham and Reading won and City finished in 19th place.

SUNDAY 12th MAY 2002

Solihull-born Darren Carter converted the vital penalty in Cardiff that ended Blues' 16-year wait for top-flight football. Birmingham City and Norwich City could not be separated at the Millennium Stadium with normal time ending goalless before Geoff Horsfield cancelled out Iwan Roberts' goal in extra time. So, for the third time in four years, Blues' promotion hopes were decided by a penalty shoot-out. Stern John, Paul Devlin and Stan Lazaridis converted Birmingham's first three spot kicks while Nico Vaesen denied Phil Mulryne and Darryl Sutch fired wide for Norwich. That left the 18-year-old Carter with the chance to send Blues into the Premier League with a nerveless penalty.

SATURDAY 13th MAY 1989

One of the worst seasons in Blues' history ended with a 4-1 defeat to Crystal Palace at Selhurst Park. Simon Sturridge scored a goal that was little consolation for a team that had already been relegated to the third tier of English football for the first time in its history.

SATURDAY 13th MAY 2000

A disastrous performance at St Andrew's saw Blues' play-off hopes go up in smoke as Barnsley won the first leg of the semi-final 4-0. Tykes winger Bruce Dyer scored twice with Neil Shipperley and Craig Hignett chipping in with a goal apiece. A much-improved Blues performance at Oakwell five days later ended in a 2-1 victory, but the damage had already been done.

SATURDAY 14th MAY 1983

Mick Harford's late goal at Coventry City secured Blues' First Division status for another season. Birmingham had gone into the final day on level points with Manchester City and just a point above Luton Town. Harford scored in the 85th minute at Highfield Road to help Blues end safely in 17th place.

TUESDAY 15th MAY 1956

Birmingham City became the first English club side to take part in European competition when they played their first group game of the 1955–58 Inter-Cities Fairs Cup. Blues visited the San Siro in Milan to take on Internazionale and came away with a 0-0 draw. Invitations to enter the tournament, which was set up to promote industrial trade fairs, were extended to the city hosting the trade fair rather than to clubs. Some cities, including London, entered a select team including players from more than one club, but Aston Villa rejected the opportunity to field a combined side.

WEDNESDAY 15th MAY 1957

Outside-right Mike Hellawell was signed from Queens Park Rangers by Birmingham City manager Arthur Turner. During a successful eight-year spell at St Andrew's Hellawell won a League Cup winners medal, appeared in the 1961 Inter-Cities Fairs Cup final and earned two England caps.

WEDNESDAY 16th MAY 1929

Roy Martin was born in Glengarnock, Ayrshire. The full-back made 74 appearances for Blues between 1950 and 1956 without ever making the position his own. Instead he provided cover for the likes of Ken Green, Jack Badham and Jeff Hall before joining Derby County.

SATURDAY 17th MAY 1924

Future Blues manager Harry Storer scored on his international debut as England beat France 3-1 in Paris.

THURSDAY 17th MAY 2001

Blues' penalty nightmares returned as they went out of the play-offs at the semi-final stage for the third year in a row. Birmingham lost a dramatic shoot-out to David Moyes' Preston North End side at Deepdale. Marcelo and Darren Purse missed City's first two penalties and Rob Edwards failed to convert for the home side before Paul McKenna scored the all-important spot kick to send Preston through. Blues led from Nicky Eaden's first-leg strike but the hosts levelled through David Healey. Geoff Horsfield put Blues back in front and it looked like it might be their night when Preston's Graham Alexander missed a penalty in normal time. However, Mark Rankine scored a dramatic late equaliser and Blues keeper Ian Bennett twice pulled off crucial saves during extra time, to deny Edwards and Healy, sending the game to penalties.

FRIDAY 18th MAY 1951

Birmingham City took on Dublin side Home Farm as part of the Festival of Britain celebrations. Blues ran out 2-1 winners in Ireland with Jackie Stewart and John Berry scoring.

SATURDAY 18th MAY 1963

A 3-2 win over Leicester City on the final day of the season averted the threat of relegation. Jimmy Harris gave Blues a first-half lead and Terry Heath pulled one back for the Foxes. However, two goals in two minutes made both the match and First Division status safe. A Bertie Auld strike and a Stan Lynn penalty made sure Birmingham finished safely two points clear of Manchester City despite Frank McLintock's late goal for Leicester.

GEOFF HORSFIELD CELEBRATES SCORING AGAINST PRESTON NORTH END

SUNDAY 19th MAY 1940

Blues beat Nottingham Forest 4-1 in a wartime match at St Andrew's. Jock Mulraney, Dave Massart, Don Dearson and guest player JB Matthews scored the Birmingham City goals.

SUNDAY 20th MAY 1951

Cork Athletic provided the opposition for Birmingham City's final match in the Festival of Britain celebrations. Cyril Trigg scored twice while Jim Higgins, Jackie Stewart and Jimmy Dailey all got a goal as Blues triumphed 5-2 in Ireland.

THURSDAY 20th MAY 1999

Birmingham City's play-off dreams ended in heartache as they lost an epic penalty shoot-out to Watford. The second leg of the play-off semi-final had got off to the perfect start as Dele Adebola scored in the 2nd minute to wipe out the Hornets' first leg advantage. Despite the loss of defender David Holdsworth, who was sent off for a second bookable offence in the 53rd minute, Birmingham dominated the match. Blues laid siege to the visitors' goal for large parts of the match but found Watford goalkeeper Alec Chamberlain in inspired form. It took 16 penalties to settle the shoot-out 7-6 with Chamberlain denying City's Paul Furlong and Chris Holland.

THURSDAY 20th MAY 2004

England striker Emile Heskey signed from Liverpool for an initial fee of £3.5m, which rose to £4.75m. Heskey's first season with Blues was a success as his 11 goals were enough to see him voted Player of the Year by both fans and his fellow players. He could only manage four goals the following season as Blues suffered relegation out of the Premier League. At the end of that campaign the striker was sold to Wigan for £5.5m.

MONDAY 21st MAY 1956

Blues recorded their first ever win in European competition with a 1-0 win over the Zagreb XI in Yugoslavia. Centre-forward Eddie Brown was the hero on the night with an 8th minute goal that was enough to separate the two sides.

MONDAY 22nd MAY 1967

Future Blues stars Bob Latchford, Dave Latchford and Garry Pendrey were part of the Birmingham City youth team that lost the second leg of the FA Youth Cup final to Sunderland at Roker Park. Blues went into the match trailing 1-0 from the first leg and lost by the same score on Wearside.

WEDNESDAY 22nd MAY 1996

Former Manchester United skipper Steve Bruce signed for Birmingham City on a free transfer. The central defender clocked up 78 Blues appearances and scored three goals over the next two seasons before taking the player-manager job at Sheffield United. Bruce returned to St Andrew's as manager in December 2001 and guided the club into the Premier League, via the play-offs, in his first season in charge.

SUNDAY 22nd MAY 2011

Blues were relegated from the Premier League on the final day of the season after losing 2-1 to Tottenham Hotspur at White Hart Lane. City were one of five sides at risk of the drop going into the match and it looked as if Craig Gardner's 79th minute equaliser would be enough to keep them safe. But, as news filtered through that Wolves were leading against Blackburn, the Blues were forced to chase the game allowing Roman Pavlyuchenko to exploit space at the back to score Spurs' second goal and condemn Blues to the drop.

THURSDAY 23rd MAY 1963

Blues took a crucial advantage in the first leg of the League Cup final with a 3-1 win over Aston Villa. Villa arrived at St Andrew's as favourites for the cup after inflicting a 4-0 derby defeat on Blues earlier in the season, which had finished with City safe from relegation by just two points. The home side turned the formbook upside down and outplayed Villa with Jimmy Harris, Bertie Auld and Ken Leek in superb attacking form. Leek scored first with Villa replying through future Blue Bobby Thomson. Leek grabbed his second before Jimmy Bloomfield added a third as Blues put one hand firmly on the League Cup trophy.

MONDAY 23rd MAY 1977

Midfielder Howard Kendall and defender Roy McDonough both scored as the 1976/77 season ended with a 2-2 draw at Queens Park Rangers. It was McDonough's only goal for Blues, in his second and final appearance for the club. He joined Walsall the following summer and in a 23-year career, with clubs including Colchester United, Southend United and Cambridge United, clocked up an English record 22 red cards.

SUNDAY 24th MAY 1959

Bunny Larkin scored twice as Blues drew 3-3 with Zagreb in the second leg of their Inter-Cities Fairs Cup quarter-final tie. Birmingham travelled to the Stadion Maksimir holding a 1-0 advantage from the home leg and Larkin's goals either side of half-time increased their lead. Although Zagreb fought back Blues scored another through Harry Hooper and progressed to the semi-final 4-3.

THURSDAY 25th MAY 1967

Former Blue Bertie Auld was one of Celtic's 'Lisbon Lions', who became the first British team to lift the European Cup, after a 2-1 victory over Internazionale in the Portuguese capital. Auld joined Blues from Celtic for £15,000 in 1961 and played in the Inter-Cities Fairs Cup final against AS Roma that year. The outside-left was part of Blues' League Cup winning side in 1963 before returning to Celtic two years later.

SUNDAY 26th MAY 1991

A spectacular John Gayle bicycle kick clinched the Leyland-DAF Cup in front of 58,756 at Wembley, as Blues saw off the challenge of Tranmere Rovers to win the competition for the first time. First-half strikes from Simon Sturridge and Gayle had put Blues in control at the break. But, Rovers hit back to level the scores and it looked as if the final was heading for extra time before Gayle's 84th minute intervention. He said, 'On the day, it just clicked for everybody. It had been a very hard season. We had a change in manager, a change round in players and it had been difficult for me. I was being slaughtered. So winning the cup was like a reward for everything we had gone through.'

SATURDAY 27th MAY 1961

Third Lanark were beaten 3-2 in New York as Blues continued their tour of the USA and Canada.

MONDAY 27th MAY 1963

An outstanding rearguard action at Villa Park secured the 1963 League Cup, the first major trophy in Birmingham City history. Blues enjoyed a 3-1 advantage going into the second leg and held Aston Villa scoreless to take the cup. Blues' captain Trevor Smith, the former England international and only survivor of the 1956 FA Cup Final, led the defensive effort and personally marked Villa danger man, and future Blue, Bobby Thomson out of the match. Villa were unable to break the defensive shackles imposed on them and City's defensive tactics paid off with a 0-0 that brought the League Cup to St Andrew's for the first time.

THURSDAY 28th MAY 1987

Former Blues skipper Garry Pendrey was appointed as the club's new manager following the departure of John Bond. Although Pendrey staved off relegation in his first season in charge he was unable to halt the team's decline. The following season began with a dreadful run of seven defeats in the first eight league games; the team never recovered and suffered relegation to the Third Division. Pendrey was replaced by Dave Mackay and despite being offered a coaching role decided to leave Birmingham City.

SATURDAY 28th MAY 2005

The original line-up of Birmingham pop legends Duran Duran performed at St Andrew's. Simon Le Bon, John Taylor, Roger Taylor, Andy Taylor and Nick Rhodes played the band's biggest show in the UK for more than 20 years at the home of the Blues. Le Bon said, 'When we played Birmingham's National Exhibition Centre while on tour earlier this year we had an amazing and very special reaction from our home town fans. It's been a while since we last played a venue of this size in the city and we are really looking forward to this very special show. We have some amazing memories of Birmingham, which is where it all started for us. Birmingham is simply our spiritual home.'

SATURDAY 29th MAY 1937

Alec Jackson was born in Tipton, Staffordshire. Jackson, who could play on the wing or at inside-forward, became West Bromwich Albion's youngest goal scorer when he hit the target on his league debut against Charlton Athletic in November 1954. A decade later he moved across the West Midlands to join Blues where he made 85 appearances across three seasons, and scored 12 goals. Jackson spent a final year at Walsall before retiring from professional football.

TUESDAY 30th MAY 1961

Blues produced easily their biggest win of the club's tour of the United States and Canada as the Calgary All Stars were thrashed 11-2 in Calgary, Alberta.

MONDAY 31st MAY 1982

Tresor Luntala was born in Kinshasa, Zaire. The midfielder played 15 times for Blues in the 2001/02 season. He went on to play for Stade Rennais in France, Grasshoppers in Switzerland and Ethnikos in Greece. Luntala was later selected to represent his country, which had changed its name to the Democratic Republic of the Congo, in the 2004 African Cup of Nations. The team lost all three of its group games finishing bottom of the table and failing to qualify for the knockout phase of the tournament.

WEDNESDAY 31st MAY 2006

Striker Cameron Jerome joined Blues in a £3m deal from Cardiff City. The England Under-21 international spent five years at St Andrew's, which took in two promotions and two relegations as well as a substitute appearance in the 2011 League Cup final. Jerome's ten goals were key to the promotion campaign of 2008/09. He began the next season in sparkling form scoring a 30-yard thunderbolt at Anfield and following it up with vital goals against Manchester United, Stoke City and Blackburn as Blues went 15 games unbeaten. His 11 goals helped City to a best Premier League finish of 9th but he could only manage three more as the club were relegated in 2010/11. In total he scored 41 goals in 201 appearances before moving to Stoke City in a £4m transfer deal in August 2011.

BIRMINGHAM CITY
On This Day

JUNE

THURSDAY 1st JUNE 1933

Harry Storer, who led Blues to the 1948 Second Division title as manager, completed his highest ever first-class cricket score for Derbyshire. Storer had been on 69 overnight, playing against Essex in the County Championship at the County Ground in Derby. He went on to score 232 out of Derbyshire's total of 455 in a match the home side won by eight wickets.

THURSDAY 1st JUNE 1972

Blues travelled to Italy and began their Anglo-Italian Cup campaign with a 0-0 draw against Lanerossi Vicenza.

SUNDAY 2nd JUNE 1935

John Metcalfe was born in Acocks Green, Birmingham. The outside-left joined Birmingham City as an amateur in 1951 and made his debut in a Second Division loss to Fulham in early 1953. At the age of 17 years and 215 days he was one of Blues' youngest ever debutants. However, he only made one more senior appearance before moving to York City in 1957.

WEDNESDAY 3rd JUNE 1896

Johnny Crosbie was born in Glenbuck, Ayrshire. Blues paid £3,000 to Ayr United in order to bring the winger south in 1920. Over the next 12 years Crosbie racked up 432 appearances for Blues, which puts him fifth on the club's all-time list. He scored 72 goals and also had a hand in many of those scored by City's record goal scorer, Joe Bradford. Crosbie won the Second Division title with Blues in 1921 and played in the FA Cup Final a decade later.

SATURDAY 3rd JUNE 1922

Frank Mitchell was born in Goulburn, New South Wales, Australia. Mitchell moved to England as a teenager and was a sporting all-rounder who played cricket for Warwickshire as well as football for Coventry City, Birmingham City and Watford. He first appeared for Blues as a guest player during World War Two and signed professional forms in 1943. The wing-half made 106 appearances for Birmingham in all competitions and scored eight goals.

THURSDAY 3rd JUNE 2004

The University of Birmingham announced that comedian and Blues fan Jasper Carrott was to receive an honorary doctorate in recognition of his 'outstanding contribution' to his chosen profession. Carrott was a director of the club between 1979 and 1982 and has a suite at St Andrew's named in his honour.

SUNDAY 4th JUNE 1972

Blues visited the Stadio Luigi Ferarris in Genoa for the second fixture of their Anglo-Italian Cup campaign. The visitors went down 2-1 to Sampdoria with Alan Campbell converting a penalty for City.

WEDNESDAY 5th JUNE 1940

As the first season of wartime football headed to a late finish Blues and Coventry City played out a 0-0 draw at St Andrew's.

WEDNESDAY 5th JUNE 1985

Frank Hodges died in Southport, Merseyside aged 94. The outside-right represented Birmingham City between 1911 and 1919 but also made wartime guest appearances for Scottish side St Mirren. He scored four goals in 27 Birmingham City matches before transferring to Manchester United.

SATURDAY 6th JUNE 1908

Birmingham City left-back Walter Corbett made his England debut as Austria were thrashed 6-1 at the Cricketer Platz in Vienna. Former Blue Jimmy Windridge scored twice as England began their first ever overseas tour with a comprehensive victory.

THURSDAY 6th JUNE 1985

Seb Larsson was born in Eskilstuna, Sweden. The midfielder initially joined Blues in 2006 on a season-long loan from Arsenal. A successful first few months at St Andrew's saw Larsson signed permanently for £1m during January 2007. As well as helping City get promoted from the Championship the Swede won the club's Goal of the Season for his goal against Sheffield Wednesday. Larsson made 204 appearances for Blues, including the League Cup final victory in 2011, and scored 25 goals. Following the club's relegation from the Premier League he joined Sunderland on a free transfer.

WEDNESDAY 7th JUNE 1961

The Victorian All Stars were thrashed 5-1 in Victoria, Canada during Blues' tour of North America.

WEDNESDAY 7th JUNE 1972

Back on home soil Blues' Anglo-Italian Cup campaign finally took off with a 5-3 victory over Lanerossi Vicenza. Bob Latchford scored twice while Trevor Francis, Bob Hatton and Gordon Taylor all grabbed a goal each.

SATURDAY 8th JUNE 1940

Blues celebrated the end of the first season of wartime football with an 8-0 demolition of Walsall at St Andrew's. Harold Bodle, Ted Duckhouse and Wilson Jones scored two goals apiece with Jackie Brown adding another. Walsall scored an own goal as Blues finished an English league season the latest in the calendar year that it has ever been completed.

WEDNESDAY 9th JUNE 1920

John Bernard Higgins scored 28 not out in Worcestershire's first innings total of 173 in a County Championship match against Sussex at Hove. Higgins was out for a duck in the second innings as Worcestershire slipped to defeat by an innings and 281 runs. Thirteen years earlier Higgins made his one and only appearance for Blues, playing at inside-left in a 1-1 draw with Chelsea in a First Division match at St Andrew's.

SATURDAY 10th JUNE 1972

Blues completed their first Anglo-Italian Cup campaign with a 2-0 victory over Sampdoria. Bob Latchford and Bob Hatton were on target against the Italian side but the result was not enough for City who finished in fourth place in the English group and were eliminated before the knockout phase of the competition began.

SATURDAY 10th JUNE 1989

Reggae superstars UB40 played a hometown gig at St Andrew's. The band played hits including 'Red Red Wine' and 'I Got You Babe'. Singer Robert Palmer also joined the band on stage for a version of 'I'll Be Your Baby Tonight'.

BOB LATCHFORD

FRIDAY 10th JUNE 2005

Finnish striker Mikael Forssell joined Blues from Chelsea in a £3m deal. The striker had first arrived at St Andrew's two seasons earlier in a loan deal and top scored for the club in the Premier League with 17 goals during the 2003/04 campaign. He returned the following season but suffered a serious knee injury. Although he recovered, and signed permanently for Blues, injuries to his other knee hampered his progress at St Andrew's. He was the club's top scorer twice more with eight in 2005/06 and nine in 2007/08 but his contribution was not enough to prevent relegation in either season.

TUESDAY 11th JUNE 1918

Walter Aveyard was born in Hemsworth, Yorkshire. The centre forward joined Blues from Sheffield Wednesday in April 1974 and made a promising start at St Andrew's. Aveyard scored three goals in his first four City matches, including one on his debut against Coventry City. However, a thigh injury curtailed his involvement and he joined Port Vale at the end of the season after playing only seven Blues games.

MONDAY 12th JUNE 1995

Birmingham City paid non-league Welling United £100,000 to secure the services of 19-year-old right-back Steve Finnan. The defender found first team opportunities limited at St Andrew's, featuring just 19 times and scoring one goal against Watford, in little over a year. After a successful loan spell at Meadow Lane he was sold to Notts County for £300,000 where he won a Third Division title. Finnan would go on to help Fulham win promotion to the Premier League before moving to Liverpool where he won the Champions League and FA Cup. He also won 53 full caps for the Republic of Ireland.

SUNDAY 12th JUNE 2011

Blues manager Alex McLeish quit the club after tendering his resignation by email. In the wake of relegation the Birmingham board had placed its confidence in McLeish as the man to lead the side back to the Premier League. However, McLeish decided to leave and five days later was controversially unveiled as the new manager of Aston Villa.

SATURDAY 13th JUNE 1908

Former Small Heath striker Jimmy Windridge equalled the England record by scoring in a sixth consecutive international when he got one of England's goals in a 4-0 win over Bohemia at the Letna Stadium in Prague. Also playing in the match was Birmingham City left-back Walter Corbett, who was winning his third and final cap.

FRIDAY 13th JUNE 1941

Tony Hateley was born in Derby. The much-travelled centre forward arrived at St Andrew's from Coventry City and in a short spell at the club scored six goals in 28 appearances before returning to Notts County where his football career had begun.

WEDNESDAY 14th JUNE 1933

Harry Hooper was born in Pittington, County Durham. The outside-forward joined Birmingham City in a £20,000 deal from Wolverhampton Wanderers in 1957. He scored 42 goals in 199 appearances for Blues over the next three years before joining Sunderland for £18,000. Hooper played in both legs of the 1960 Inter-Cities Fairs Cup final and scored City's consolation goal at the Camp Nou in Barcelona.

TUESDAY 15th JUNE 1965

St Andrew's hosted championship boxing as Henry Cooper successfully defended his British and Empire Heavyweight title. Cooper beat the challenger Johnny Prescott by technical knockout in the 10th round.

SUNDAY 16th JUNE 1929

Alex Govan was born in Glasgow, Scotland. Blues boss Bob Brocklebank brought the outside-left to St Andrew's from Plymouth Argyle for £6,500 in June 1953. Govan was reluctant to move from the south coast but Brocklebank lured him to Birmingham with the promise of a house. He became an integral part of the Birmingham forward line that won promotion and reached the FA Cup Final in the 1950s. He is also credited with introducing Sir Harry Lauder's 'Keep Right on to the End of the Road' to Birmingham City, which became the club's unofficial anthem on the road to Wembley in 1956 and has been a fan favourite ever since. He was elected to Blues' Hall of Fame in 2012.

MONDAY 16th JUNE 2008

Central midfielder Fabrice Muamba was sold to Bolton Wanderers for £5m. The England Under-21 international first arrived at St Andrew's on loan in 2006. An impressive first season with Blues saw him help the club get promoted. He was also voted Young Player of the Year by fans and offered a contract by Birmingham who paid Arsenal £4m for his services. He made 37 appearances the following season but was unable to prevent the club's immediate return to the Championship and moved to Bolton. In 2012 he suffered a heart attack on the pitch was subsequently forced to retire from football.

THURSDAY 17th JUNE 1954

Gil Merrick became the first Blue to play in the World Cup finals when he was selected to play in goal for England's opening match in Switzerland. The match against Belgium at the St Jakob Stadium in Basel ended 4-4 with Ivor Broadis and Nat Lofthouse sharing two goals each for England. Although this was a group stage game it went to extra time, the first time an England game had done so.

SATURDAY 17th JUNE 2006

Scottish midfielder Barry Ferguson was made a Member of the Order of the British Empire for services to football in the Queen's Birthday Honours list. At the time Ferguson had won 33 Scotland caps, he would add another 12 later, and led Rangers to two Scottish titles. In July 2009 his old Rangers boss Alex McLeish brought him to St Andrew's in a £1m deal. The following season Ferguson won the club's Players' Player of the Year award. He played in 82 Blues matches, including the 2011 League Cup final, which he finished with a broken rib.

MONDAY 18th JUNE 1928

Stan Lynn was born in Bolton, Lancashire. The full-back was known as 'Stan the Wham' due to his powerful dead-ball exploits. Lynn began his career with Accrington Stanley before spending over a decade at Aston Villa. He crossed the city to join Blues for £15,000 in 1961. At St Andrew's he scored 30 goals in 148 appearances and won the League Cup.

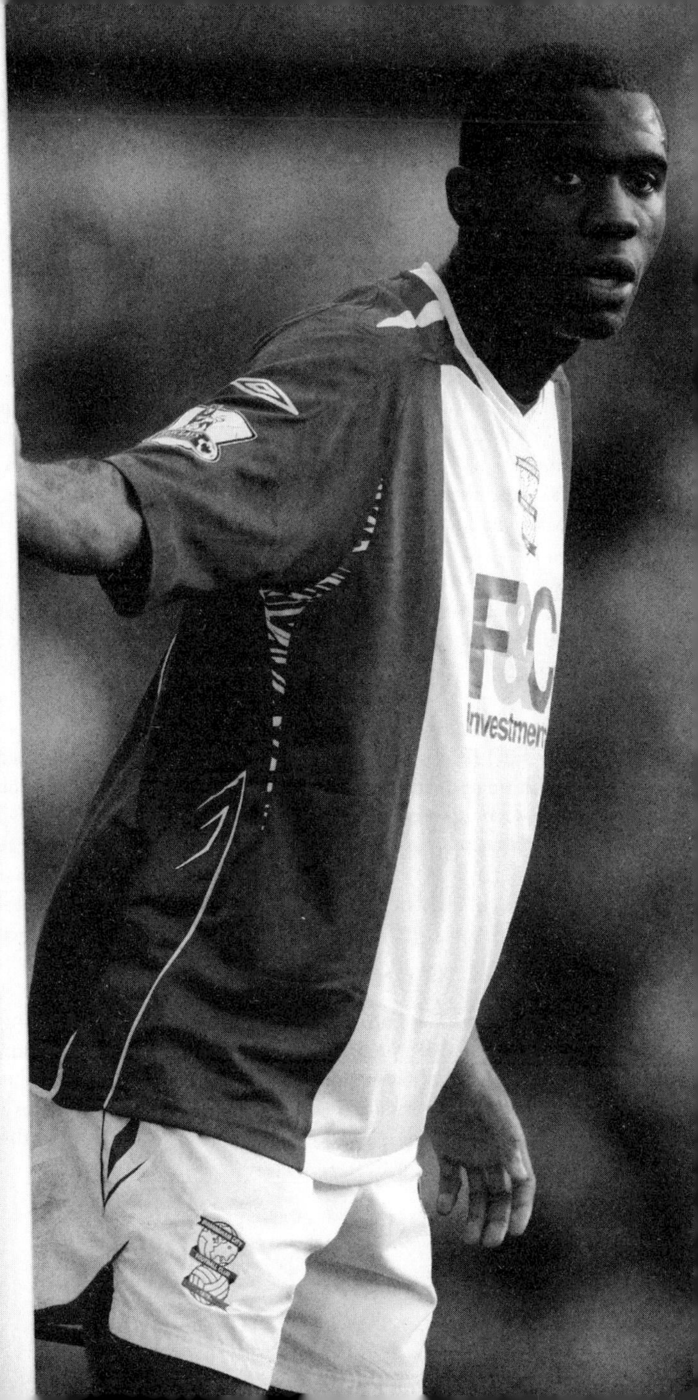

FABRICE MUAMBA

TUESDAY 18th JUNE 1991

Blues manager Lou Macari left the club to take over at Stoke City. Macari had been appointed on a non-contract basis the previous January with the club in a perilous situation on and off the pitch. Blues were in danger of dropping down to the fourth tier for the first time in their history and in dire straits financially. The former Celtic and Manchester United midfielder steadied the ship, guiding the team to a 15th place finish as well as winning the Leyland-DAF Cup at Wembley. Macari said, 'When I took over the Birmingham job without any contract, things were so bad the chairman asked me to raise £250,000 by the end of the season. It looked impossible, but the revenue was delivered with the great run in the Leyland-DAF. It's no secret that, if we hadn't got to Wembley, Birmingham would have been in financial trouble and might have gone under.'

TUESDAY 19th JUNE 1917

Doug Pimbley was born in Kings Norton, Birmingham. The forward joined Birmingham City in July 1946. Pimbley only made two appearances for Blues before he was transferred to Notts County.

SATURDAY 19th JUNE 1976

Bryan Hughes was born in Liverpool, Merseyside. The midfielder made his name during Wrexham's run to the FA Cup quarter-finals in 1997 earning himself a £1m move to St Andrew's. Hughes spent the next seven seasons with Blues making 293 appearances and scoring 42 goals. He was a key member of the team that returned the club to the top flight in 2002. Hughes also appeared as a substitute in the 2001 League Cup final and converted a penalty in the shoot-out.

WEDNESDAY 20th JUNE 1934

Graham Leggat was born in Aberdeen, Scotland. The right-winger won the Scottish league title and League Cup with his hometown club as well as representing his country at the 1958 World Cup finals in Sweden. Leggat headed south making over 250 appearances for Fulham before a brief spell with Birmingham City. He scored three goals in 20 outings for Blues.

MONDAY 20th JUNE 1949

St Andrew's hosted championship boxing as Dick Turpin successfully defended his British Empire middleweight title with a points victory over Albert Finch. Fighting on the undercard was Turpin's younger brother Randolph, who beat Belgian middleweight Cyrille Delannoit by a technical knockout. Randolph would go on to win the World middleweight title with a famous victory over Sugar Ray Robinson in 1951.

SUNDAY 20th JUNE 1982

Blues legend Trevor Francis opened the scoring in England's group match against Czechoslovakia at the 1982 World Cup finals in Spain. Francis volleyed home from a Ray Wilkins corner in the 62nd minute and four minutes later Jozef Barmos slid the ball past his own keeper to make it 2-0.

WEDNESDAY 21st JUNE 1978

Alberto Tarantini was amongst the scorers as hosts Argentina brushed aside Peru 6-0 in a second-round Group B match in the 1978 World Cup. Four months after the tournament the attack-minded full-back signed for Blues from Boca Juniors for £259,000. His home debut attracted a crowd of 36,000 to St Andrew's – double the previous match – but he never settled in England and his contract was cancelled after just 24 games and one goal.

TUESDAY 22nd JUNE 1965

Bob Catlin was born in Wembley, London. The goalkeeper was brought up in Australia but returned to his native country to play for Notts County. He joined Blues on loan in 1993 and completed eight matches for City despite it transpiring that the club had actually scouted a different Magpies goalkeeper.

WEDNESDAY 22nd JUNE 2011

Chris Hughton was appointed as Birmingham City's manager. The former Spurs and Republic of Ireland defender had led Newcastle United to the Championship title a year earlier. Hughton led Blues to the group stage of the Europa League and was named the Championship Manager of the Month for October. In the league his side finished 4th before going out of the play-offs to Blackpool.

MONDAY 23rd JUNE 1975

Bamberdele Olusegun Adebola was born in Lagos, Nigeria. Adebola, who is usually known as Dele, moved to Liverpool as a child and progressed through the youth system at Crewe Alexandra. City manager Trevor Francis signed him for Blues for a fee of £1m in February 1998. Adebola scored seven goals in the remainder of that season and another 17 the following season to finish as the club's top scorer and help them to a 3rd place finish in the First Division. His goals were also key during the run to the 2001 League Cup final. Despite suffering from injuries during his stay at St Andrew's the striker managed 41 goals in 154 appearances before leaving for Crystal Palace.

SUNDAY 24th JUNE 2007

Jonathan Spector was part of the United States team that won the CONCACAF Gold Cup with a 2-1 victory over Mexico at Soldier Field in Chicago. A Landon Donovan penalty levelled the scores after Mexico took a first-half lead and Benny Feilhaber hit the winning goal after 73 minutes. Spector would join Blues from West Ham United on a free transfer in 2011. The versatile Spector could play in defence or midfield and made 179 appearances for Birmingham City before returning to the US in January 2017.

SUNDAY 25th JUNE 1978

Alberto Tarantini, who joined Blues the following October, was part of the Argentina team that won the 1978 World Cup final on home soil with a 3-1 victory over the Netherlands in Buenos Aires.

FRIDAY 25th JUNE 1982

Trevor Francis scored for the second World Cup match in a row as England saw off the challenge of Kuwait 1-0 in Bilbao.

TUESDAY 25th JUNE 2013

Blues defender Curtis Davies joined Hull City in a £2.25m transfer deal. The former West Bromwich Albion and Aston Villa player had arrived two years earlier on a free transfer. Davies played 106 matches for Blues and scored 12 goals before moving to the Tigers.

TUESDAY 26th JUNE 2001

Ray Devey died in Birmingham, aged 83. The centre-half turned professional with Blues in 1937 but had his career progression interrupted by the outbreak of World War Two. Devey played in nine wartime fixtures for Blues before finally making his league debut in 1946. He retired from playing following spells with Mansfield Town and Hereford United and returned to St Andrew's, where he held a number of roles including coach, trainer, physiotherapist and kit man.

SUNDAY 26th JUNE 2016

Former Blues midfielder Jean Beausejour scored a penalty in the shoot-out as Chile won their second successive Copa America. Argentina were beaten 4-2 on penalties after a goalless match at the Met Life Stadium in New Jersey. Alex McLeish signed Beausejour from Mexican side America in August 2010 following the player's impressive World Cup campaign for Chile. In 18 months at St Andrew's he appeared in 56 matches and scored five goals in all competitions.

TUESDAY 27th JUNE 1922

Tommy Capel was born in Chorlton-on-Medlock, Manchester. The inside-left followed manager Bob Brocklebank from Chesterfield to Blues for a £10,000 transfer fee in 1949. Capel failed to settle in Birmingham and moved on to Nottingham Forest later that year after making just eight appearances and scoring one goal.

WEDNESDAY 28th JUNE 1933

Freddie Goodwin was born in Heywood, Lancashire. Playing as wing-half Goodwin won consecutive league titles with Manchester United in 1956 and 1957. He turned to management after a triple leg break, the result of a collision with John Charles, ended his playing career. Goodwin arrived at St Andrew's in 1970, via spells at Scunthorpe United and Brighton & Hove Albion, to replace Stan Cullis. His five years in charge of Blues saw promotion to the First Division in 1972 as well as two appearances in the FA Cup semi-finals. Goodwin gave Trevor Francis his Blues debut and introduced modern training techniques including psychology and yoga to the club. A sporting all-rounder Goodwin also played first-class cricket and made 11 appearances for Lancashire as a fast-medium bowler.

SUNDAY 28th JUNE 2009

Jonathan Spector provided the assist for Clint Dempsey to open the scoring for the US in the FIFA Confederations Cup final against Brazil in South Africa. Despite taking a two-goal lead when Landon Donovan added another the US would go on to lose the final 3-2 to the South Americans. Luis Fabiano scored twice for Brazil with Lucio scoring an 84th minute winner at Ellis Park in Johannesburg. Two years later Spector would join Blues from West Ham United.

SATURDAY 29th JUNE 1929

Future Blues manager Harry Storer scored 209 runs as he and his opening partner Joseph Bowden put on 322 for the first wicket when Derbyshire met Essex in the County Championship. The score remains the Derbyshire record for a first-wicket stand.

WEDNESDAY 29th JUNE 2011

Birmingham City owner Carson Yeung was arrested at his home in Hong Kong in connection with alleged money laundering. Yeung went on trial two years later and was convicted on five counts of money laundering.

THURSDAY 30th JUNE 1938

Mike Hellawell was born in Keighley, Yorkshire. The outside-right joined Blues from Queens Park Rangers in May 1957 and stayed at St Andrew's for eight seasons. During that time he won a League Cup winners' tankard, played in the Inter-Cities Fairs Cup final against Roma, won two England caps and made an appearance for Warwickshire County Cricket Club. Hellawell scored 33 goals in 213 Blues appearances before joining Sunderland.

THURSDAY 30th JUNE 2011

Midfielder Craig Gardner moved to Sunderland in a £6m deal. Gardner had arrived at St Andrew's from Villa Park 18 months earlier for £3m. In his one full season at the club Gardner top scored with eight Premier League goals plus two in cup competitions. It was his extra-time strike against West Ham United that sent Blues to Wembley for the 2011 League Cup final. Gardner returned to Birmingham City in January 2017 on a loan deal from West Bromwich Albion.

BIRMINGHAM CITY
On This Day

JULY

SUNDAY 1st JULY 1877

Jack Aston was born in Walsall, Staffordshire. The inside-forward began his professional career with his hometown club and arrived at Small Heath in 1900 via a short spell at Woolwich Arsenal. The high point of his three seasons with Blues was 1900/01 when he scored 12 goals during the club's promotion campaign. Overall he scored 24 goals in 61 appearances for Small Heath.

SUNDAY 1st JULY 1923

Blues beat Spanish giants Real Madrid 3-0 in a pre-season friendly in Spain, despite finishing with 10 men. Birmingham City's Alec McClure was sent off for gamesmanship after taking his protests at the award of a penalty to Real too far.

SUNDAY 2nd JULY 2000

Christophe Dugarry was in the starting line-up of the France team that beat Italy 2-1 to win Euro 2000. The French team became the first in history to hold both the World Cup and the European Championship, after David Trezeguet's golden goal gave them victory in the final at De Kuip in Rotterdam. Three years later Dugarry joined Blues and played a key role in maintaining the side's Premier League status. In all he played 31 times and scored six goals for Blues before retiring from competitive football.

TUESDAY 3rd JULY 1962

Warwickshire completed a 161-run victory over Oxford University at Edgbaston. Making his only first class appearance for Warwickshire was Blues outside-right Mike Hellawell, who made 59 runs and took six wickets in the match.

THURSDAY 3rd JULY 1975

Lee Bradbury was born in Cowes, Isle of Wight. The striker joined Blues on loan from Crystal Palace and played seven games in the league as well as both legs against Watford in the play-offs. Bradbury never scored for Blues, although he did convert a penalty during the unsuccessful shoot-out against the Hornets at St Andrew's.

THURSDAY 3rd JULY 2003

Blues transfer record was broken when the club paid out £5.5m to sign midfielder David Dunn from Blackburn Rovers. Although Dunn's Blues career started brightly, with a debut goal against Tottenham Hotspur, his three seasons at St Andrew's were blighted by a recurring hamstring problem. The midfielder was restricted to 59 appearances in all competitions during his time at the club. He returned to Ewood Park for a fee of £2.2m during the January 2007 transfer window.

MONDAY 4th JULY 2005

Darren Carter signed for West Bromwich Albion in a £2.5m transfer deal. The Solihull-born midfielder wrote his name into Blues' history by converting the penalty that ended a 16-year wait for top-flight football and took the club into the Premier League for the first time. Carter made his Birmingham debut in January 2002 and within four months he had played a vital role in the play-off win over Norwich City in Cardiff. His Premier League career with Blues was a stop-start affair and although he enjoyed his best season in 2004/05, with 27 appearances and two goals, he moved to The Hawthorns at the end of the campaign.

SATURDAY 4th JULY 2015

Former Blues midfielder Jean Beausejour was part of the Chile side that beat Argentina in the Copa America final. The match took place at the Estadio Nacional in Santiago and finished goalless after extra time. Chile won their first Copa America title with a 4-1 victory in the penalty shoot-out.

FRIDAY 5th JULY 1991

Regulators from seven countries raided the offices of the Bank Of Credit and Commerce International (BCCI) around the world. The bank was declared insolvent amidst accusations of fraud, money laundering and other financial irregularities. Amidst the fallout from the collapse of BCCI was the calling in of loans that put the clothing business of Birmingham owners the Kumar brothers into receivership. The brothers were forced to sell their 84% stake in the Blues and after a four-month spell in administration the club was bought by David Sullivan and the Gold brothers.

SATURDAY 6th JULY 2002

St Andrew's hosted pop music festival Party in the Park. Gareth Gates headlined the concert, which was attended by 30,000 music fans, while boy bands Westlife and Blue also appeared on stage.

THURSDAY 6th JULY 2006

Ex-France, Paris Saint-Germain and AC Milan defender Bruno N'Gotty signed a one-year contract with Birmingham City after arriving on a free transfer from Bolton Wanderers. N'Gotty played 25 matches in the Championship for Blues, helping them to return to the Premier League at the first attempt, before joining Leicester City.

TUESDAY 7th JULY 1903

'Diamond' Freddie Wheldon's innings of 112 for Worcestershire against Somerset at New Road was his highest ever first-class score. His runs helped Worcestershire to a huge total of 590 as they won the match by an innings and 109 runs.

FRIDAY 7th JULY 2006

Striker Emile Heskey was sold to Premier League Wigan Athletic for £5.5m, the third highest transfer fee Birmingham City have received for a player. The England striker spent two seasons at St Andrew's after arriving from Liverpool in a £3.5m deal. He scored 16 goals in 78 matches but was allowed to leave following the club's relegation.

TUESDAY 8th JULY 1969

Adrian Bird was born in Bristol. The centre-back joined Blues as an apprentice and made his debut at the age of 17 in a Second Division match against Millwall in December 1987. He made 31 appearances for Blues over the next three seasons and scored a goal against Wolves in a League Cup match. Unfortunately, a knee injury forced Bird to retire from football at the age of just 21.

SATURDAY 8th JULY 2006

Striker DJ Campbell scored four goals and set up another for Cameron Jerome as Burton Albion were swept aside 5-1 in a pre-season friendly at the Pirelli Stadium.

EMILE HESKEY

FRIDAY 9th JULY 1869

Frank Richards was born in Amblecote, Staffordshire. He was appointed as Birmingham City secretary in 1910 and was responsible for team affairs for eight years from 1915. Richards signed record-scorer Joe Bradford and oversaw the Second Division title campaign in 1921.

WEDNESDAY 9th JULY 2008

Former Aston Villa and West Bromwich Albion striker Kevin Phillips joined Blues on a free transfer. The England international scored the winner on his City debut after coming on as a sub against Sheffield United and hit another 13 goals to help Alex McLeish's side gain promotion to the Premier League. McLeish often used Phillips as a sub, he made 37 starts for Birmingham, but came off the bench 45 times in his three seasons at St Andrew's. He scored 22 goals in all competitions for Blues with late strikes earning a memorable victory over Wolverhampton Wanderers and a draw against Arsenal in the Premier League.

MONDAY 10th JULY 2000

Blues manager Trevor Francis broke the club's transfer record when he signed striker Geoff Horsfield from Fulham for £2.25m. In three eventful years with Birmingham the Barnsley-born striker would score 29 goals in 126 appearances. These included two strikes in a League Cup semi-final, an extra-time equaliser in the play-off final against Norwich and goals home and away against Villa in the top flight. In the second of those Second City derby matches Horsfield ended the match in goal following an injury to regular keeper Nico Vaesen, which occurred after Blues had used all their substitutions.

MONDAY 11th JULY 1892

Joe Lane was born in Hereford, England. The nomadic striker played for Ferencvaros in Hungary, Sunderland and Blackpool before arriving at Birmingham City for a club record transfer fee of £3,600. The mercurial marksman, who was famed for conjuring scoring opportunities from unpromising situations, scored 26 times in 67 Blues appearances. His goals included a hat-trick in a 7-0 demolition of Lincoln City shortly after joining the club. It was his second treble of the season against the Imps having already tormented them in Blackpool's earlier that campaign.

MONDAY 11th JULY 2011

Blues central defender Roger Johnson signed for Wolverhampton Wanderers for an undisclosed fee, although reports suggested the deal was worth around £5m. Johnson had arrived from Cardiff City two years earlier and enjoyed a stellar first season at St Andrew's. His partnership with Scott Dann in the heart of Blues' defence was a key reason for the club's 6th place Premier League finish. He also played a vital role in the 2011 League Cup success but was unable to help the club avoid the drop. Following his move to Wolves he endured relegation twice more.

SUNDAY 12th JULY 1998

Future Birmingham striker Christophe Dugarry came on as a 66th-minute substitute as France won the World Cup final on home soil, with a one-sided 3-0 victory over Brazil. Two Zinedine Zidane headers and a late strike from Arsenal's Emmanuel Petit clinched the trophy at the Stade de France in Paris. The build-up to the match had been overshadowed by the omission of Ronaldo from the Brazilian line-up and although the striker played he was a shadow of his usual self.

SUNDAY 13th JULY 1952

Birmingham City took on Aston Villa in a one-day cricket match played for the benefit of Warwickshire bowler Tom Pritchard. The match at the Wolseley Motors Athletic Ground in Birmingham ended in a draw. Blues batted first and racked up 163 as South African-born forward Ted Purdon top scored with 105. Warwickshire batsman Tom Cartwright led the Villa reply, scoring 70 out of the total of 149-7 scored when play ended for the day. City's wickets were shared between Dennis Jennings with four and Gil Merrick with three.

WEDNESDAY 13th JULY 2016

George Allen died in Solihull aged 84. Although the left-back was born in Small Heath he arrived at St Andrew's via a spell at Coventry City. Allen played in 165 Birmingham City matches spread over ten years but never scored a goal. He lost his place after fracturing his skull in 1961 and moved to Torquay United the following year.

SUNDAY 14th JULY 1895

George Liddell was born in Murton, County Durham. Liddell joined Blues from South Shields in 1920 and spent 12 seasons representing the club at wing-half and full-back. He played 345 matches in all competitions, including the 1931 FA Cup Final against West Bromwich Albion, and scored six Blues goals. After hanging up his boots he took over as City manager from Leslie Knighton, a role he held for six years from July 1933, which is the longest period of time that one person has managed to hold the job. Throughout his tenure the club flirted with relegation from the top flight and the team eventually suffered the drop in 1939.

MONDAY 14th JULY 1997

Coventry City winger Peter Ndlovu joined Birmingham City in a £1.6m deal. The Zimbabwe international was popular amongst the Blues faithful during his four-year spell at St Andrew's, twice helping the side to reach the play-offs. Ndlovu scored 27 goals in 101 Blues starts but was loaned to Huddersfield Town in 2000 before moving to Sheffield United a year later.

WEDNESDAY 15th JULY 1953

Alan Ainscow was born in Bolton, Lancashire. Birmingham City paid a transfer fee of £40,000 to Blackpool to secure the midfielder's services in 1978. He scored 22 goals in 125 appearances over the next three years. Ainscow was part of the Blues side that won promotion from the Second Division in 1980 and a year later he joined Everton in a £250,000 deal.

SATURDAY 16th JULY 2011

Ex-Blues midfielder Curtis Woodhouse challenged Birmingham-born Frankie Gavin for the WBO Inter-Continental title at the Echo Arena in Liverpool. Gavin won the 12-round bout by a split decision to retain his championship belt. Before turning professional as a boxer Woodhouse had made a name for himself as a footballer at York City and Sheffield United, winning England Under-21 caps while at Bramall Lane. He joined Birmingham City for £1m in February 2001 and made 45 appearances over the next three seasons, scoring two goals, before leaving for Peterborough United on a free transfer.

PETER NDLOVU

WEDNESDAY 17th JULY 1996

Birmingham City broke the million pound barrier for the first time when striker Paul Furlong was signed from Chelsea for £1.5m. Furlong was one of Trevor Francis' 'Premier League Gang of Five' along with Steve Bruce, Mike Newell, Barry Horne and Gary Ablett. The signings all had top-flight experience and were recruited in order to take Blues to the Premier League. Furlong's best season in terms of goals was 1997/98 when he notched 19, but it was not enough to secure promotion. In all he spent six seasons at St Andrew's scoring 56 goals in 156 games for Blues before departing for Loftus Road.

SATURDAY 18th JULY 2015

A late goal from ex-Villa defender Shane Lowry saved City's blushes in a pre-season friendly against Kidderminster Harriers at Aggborough. The home side had taken the lead in the 68th minute after Adam Dawson had cashed in on a poor Tomasz Kuszczak clearance. That goal looked like it might be enough for the Harriers as Blues wasted several good chances. But with eight minutes left Lowry rose at the back post to head home Stephen Gleeson's free kick. Although Lowry's trial period with Birmingham led to him being offered a contract he would only play one league game for the club before it was cancelled by mutual consent and he returned to his native Australia.

THURSDAY 19th JULY 1928

Bobby Davidson was born in Airdrie, North Lanarkshire. The referee took charge of the first leg of the 1961 Inter-Cities Fairs Cup final between Blues and Roma and was praised for a strong performance in the face of the Italian side's antics.

MONDAY 19th JULY 1982

Stuart Parnaby was born in Durham, County Durham. In June 2007 manager Steve Bruce brought the England Under-21 right-back to St Andrew's from Middlesbrough on a free transfer. Parnaby's best season with Blues was 2008/09 when he made 21 Championship appearances as the club gained promotion. In all he made 62 appearances for Blues and scored one goal, in a 3-2 FA Cup victory over Coventry City.

FRIDAY 20th JULY 2007

Blues striker DJ Campbell was sold to Leicester City for an initial fee of £1.6m. Campbell had joined Blues from Brentford 18 months earlier in a £600,000 deal. After a slow start to his St Andrew's career the striker had found the back of the net nine times during City's successful promotion campaign in 2006/07.

SATURDAY 21st JULY 1984

Liam Ridgewell was born in Bexleyheath, Kent. The defender began his youth career with West Ham United before moving to Villa Park where he won the FA Youth Cup in 2002. In 2007 Ridgewell became the first player to move between Aston Villa and Birmingham for over 20 years when he joined Blues in a £2m deal. In five years at St Andrew's Ridgewell made 152 appearances and scored nine times.

THURSDAY 22nd JULY 1909

Jimmy Windridge scored 23 out of Warwickshire's total of 199 against Yorkshire in a three-day County Championship match at Headingley in Leeds. Windridge was born in Small Heath and turned professional with Blues in 1901. The inside-forward played a part in Small Heath's 1903 promotion campaign and was sold to Chelsea for £190 in 1905. He won England caps while at Chelsea and returned to Birmingham in 1914, after a stint at Middlesbrough. Over his two spells at the club Windridge clocked up 61 appearances and scored 19 goals.

WEDNESDAY 22nd JULY 1998

Premier League Tottenham Hotspur were beaten 4-2 in a pre-season friendly by Trevor Francis' Birmingham team. Dele Adebola scored twice against Spurs with Paul Furlong and Jon McCarthy also hitting the back of the net.

FRIDAY 23rd JULY 1965

Keith Downing was born in Oldbury, West Midlands. The midfielder arrived at Blues from Wolves on a free transfer in 1993 but failed to make an impact at St Andrew's. After making just one league appearance, and another in the League Cup, he moved on to Stoke City in August 1994.

TUESDAY 24th JULY 1888

Small Heath Alliance became the first football club to incorporate as a limited company, with share capital of £650, and introduce a board of directors. Walter Hart was the club's first chairman and he announced that the word 'Alliance' had been dropped from the name of Small Heath Football Club Ltd.

WEDNESDAY 24th JULY 1996

Canadian striker Paul Peschisolido left Birmingham City for the second time, joining West Bromwich Albion in a £600,000 deal. Peschisolido arrived at Birmingham City from Toronto Blizzards in August 1992 in a £25,000 transfer. He scored 17 goals in 48 appearances and was joint top scorer in both of his full seasons at the club. After a spell at Stoke City he returned in March 1996 playing nine more Blues matches and adding another goal to his tally before leaving for The Hawthorns.

SATURDAY 25th JULY 1998

Zimbabwe international striker Peter Ndlovu scored a hat-trick as Blues beat Manchester United 4-3 in a pre-season friendly.

FRIDAY 26th JULY 1935

Ken Leek was born in Ynysybwl, Wales. The Welsh international forward was signed from Newcastle United for £23,000 in November 1961 and scored his first two Blues goals against Cardiff City the following month. Over the next three and half years he scored 61 goals in 120 Blues appearances. The highlight was his double in the first leg of the 1963 League Cup final that set City on course for their first major trophy. The following year he returned to his first professional club, Northampton Town, for a transfer fee of £10,000. Leek also won 13 Wales caps and scored five goals for his country. He is the grandfather of Karl Darlow who has played in goal for Nottingham Forest and Newcastle United.

FRIDAY 26th JULY 1996

Blues manager Barry Fry used 21 players in a pre-season friendly against Walsall. Birmingham won the match 2-1 thanks to late goals from Paul Harding and Carl Shutt.

WEDNESDAY 26th JULY 2006

Winger Jermaine Pennant became the most expensive player ever sold by Birmingham City when Liverpool paid a transfer fee of £6.7m to take him to Anfield. Steve Bruce signed Pennant from Arsenal in 2005 following a loan spell, with the club standing by the player despite his conviction for driving offences. The winger scored three times on 60 appearances for Blues who accepted Liverpool's record bid after suffering relegation from the Premier League.

WEDNESDAY 27th JULY 2016

Teenager Jack Storer came off the bench to complete a pre-season friendly victory against Port Vale. The 18-year-old gave Blues the lead with a powerful header and a Paul Caddis penalty wrapped up a 2-0 win at Vale Park.

THURSDAY 28th JULY 1910

Former player Bob McRoberts was appointed as Blues' first full-time manager at the club's annual meeting. Prior to McRoberts' appointment the committee selected the team but the Scot took over team affairs and brought in former Aston Villa and England goalkeeper Billy George as his assistant. McRoberts held the post until the outbreak of World War One before retiring.

WEDNESDAY 28th JULY 1999

Australian international Stan Lazaridis signed from West Ham United in a £1.5m deal. Lazaridis, who could play at left-wing or left-back, was a key member of the side that won promotion to the Premier League in 2003 and converted a penalty in the play-off final in Cardiff. He also appeared in the 2001 League Cup final. In seven years he made 224 appearances for Blues and scored eight goals before returning to his native Australia to join Perth Glory.

SATURDAY 29th JULY 1933

Brian Farmer was born in Wordsley, Staffordshire. The right-back joined City as a 17-year-old in 1950 and made his first team debut six years later. Farmer played in 145 matches for Blues, including two Inter-Cities Fairs Cup finals, without ever scoring a goal. He left for Bournemouth & Boscombe Athletic in 1962.

FRIDAY 29th JULY 1983

Birmingham City ventured 100 miles north of the Arctic Circle for a pre-season friendly with Swedish club Gallivare. Blues lost 2-1 with winger Robert Hopkins scoring for the visitors.

MONDAY 29th JULY 2013

Christian Benitez died in Doha, Qatar aged 27. The Ecuadorian striker's performances in helping El Nacional win the title in his home country and Santos Laguna win the Mexican championship earned him a move to St Andrew's in 2009. Although initial reports suggested he could become Blues' biggest transfer, with fees rising to a possible £9m, the deal was almost derailed when his medical revealed knee problems. The striker scored four goals and showed glimpses of his potential during his spell in Birmingham before returning to Mexico in 2010. He joined Qatari club El Jaish in July 2013 but died of a cardiac arrest less than 24 hours after playing his first match for the team.

SATURDAY 30th JULY 1966

Future Birmingham City director and manager Sir Alf Ramsey guided England to World Cup final victory. England beat West Germany 4-2 at after extra time at Wembley Stadium thanks to a Geoff Hurst hat-trick and a Martin Peters goal.

TUESDAY 30th JULY 2002

Blues manager Steve Bruce broke the club's transfer record when he signed Clinton Morrison from Crystal Palace for £4.25m, with striker Andrew Johnson moving the other way as part of the deal. A goal in the derby victory over Aston Villa during his first season at the club was the highlight of Morrison's time at the club. He managed 16 goals in 97 appearances spread over three seasons before returning to Selhurst Park for £2m.

SUNDAY 31st JULY 1983

Blues ran out easy 2-0 winners against Ranea on their pre-season tour of Swedish Lapland. Ian Handysides and Mick Harford scored twice each with full-back Pat Van Den Hauwe also finding the back of the net.

BIRMINGHAM CITY
On This Day

AUGUST

MONDAY 1st AUGUST 1983

England youth international Nigel Winterburn was allowed to leave Birmingham City for Oxford United on a free transfer. Although the full-back never made a senior appearance for either Blues or Oxford he went on to make a name for himself at Wimbledon. Winterburn helped the Crazy Gang win promotion to the top flight before moving to Arsenal. At Arsenal he won three league titles, two FA Cups and the League Cup as well as the European Cup Winners' Cup and two England caps.

SATURDAY 1st AUGUST 2015

A minute's silence was observed at St Andrew's in memory of Denis Thwaites before Birmingham City's friendly against Leicester City. The former City player was murdered along with his wife Elaine in the terrorist attack at a Tunisian resort two months earlier. The couple were amongst the 38 tourists killed by a gunman in Sousse. The outside-left played 95 matches for City and won the League Cup in 1963.

WEDNESDAY 2nd AUGUST 1893

The Second Division championship shield, won the previous season, was presented to Small Heath at a meeting of the Football League, which was held at the Colonnade Hotel in New Street.

WEDNESDAY 3rd AUGUST 1983

Ian Handysides scored as Blues' tour of Sweden continued with a 1-0 victory over Alvsbyn to make it two wins in a row.

THURSDAY 4th AUGUST 1870

Sir Harry Lauder was born in Edinburgh, Scotland. Lauder was a music hall composer, singer and comedian known for songs such as *I Love Lassie* and *Roamin' in the Gloamin'*. Lauder was the first Scottish artist to sell a million records and his music became part of the war effort for World War One. Winston Churchill said that Lauder 'by his inspiring songs and valiant life, rendered measureless service… to the British Empire'. He wrote *Keep Right On To the End of the Road* following the death of his son during the war, which has since become a fans' anthem at St Andrew's.

SATURDAY 5th AUGUST 1972

Blues triumphed in the first penalty shoot-out in FA Cup history to beat Stoke City in the 3rd/4th place play-off. The two sides were goalless after both 90 minutes and extra time, so had to be separated by spot kicks. Blues edged the shoot-out 4-3 with Alan Campbell, Trevor Francis, Bobby Hope and Stan Harland all on target from 12 yards. The play-off was introduced in 1970 for the losers of the previous season's semi-finals, but proved unpopular and only lasted for five seasons.

FRIDAY 5th AUGUST 1994

Terry Hibbitt died in Newcastle upon Tyne, aged 46. The midfielder made his name with Newcastle United before moving to St Andrew's in 1975. In his three years with Blues Hibbitt made 122 appearances and scored 11 goals before returning to the Magpies.

SATURDAY 5th AUGUST 2006

Blues made a winning start as they attempted to bounce straight back to the Premier League beating Colchester United 2-1 at St Andrew's. Striker DJ Campbell scored his first league goal for the club to open the scoring with Arsenal loanee Nicklas Bendtner adding the second. However, striker Cameron Jerome had a debut to forget when he was sent off for elbowing an opponent just five minutes after coming on as a substitute.

SATURDAY 6th AUGUST 2011

A stunning drive from Derby County's Steve Davies completed the Rams' comeback and condemned Blues to defeat on their return to the Championship. Defender Curtis Davies had given Birmingham an early lead at Pride Park heading home from a corner after 19 minutes. Jason Shackell levelled for the home side before Davies struck just before half-time. Blues might have taken a point but Stephen Carr smashed a golden opportunity over the bar.

SUNDAY 7th AUGUST 1983

Blues completed their tour of Northern Sweden with an emphatic 5-0 victory over Haparanda. Jamaican defender Noel Blake scored twice with Robert Hopkins, Les Phillips and Billy Wright also on target.

THURSDAY 7th AUGUST 1986

Goalkeeper David Seaman was sold to Queens Park Rangers for £225,000. Yorkshire-born Seaman had joined Birmingham from Peterborough United in October 1984 and his two seasons at the club had encompassed both a promotion and a relegation during which time he made 75 appearances for Blues. Four years later he was sold to Arsenal for £1.3m, a record fee for a goalkeeper. At Arsenal Seaman won three League titles, four FA Cups, the League Cup and the European Cup Winners' Cup. He also won 75 England caps and played in four major tournaments with the national team.

SATURDAY 7th AUGUST 1999

Stan Lazaridis' stunning late free kick ensured Blues gained a point on the opening day of the season despite having trailed by two goals to Fulham. Future Blue Geoff Horsfield had scored both goals for the Cottagers before seeing red. Midfielder Bryan Hughes pulled a goal back then Lazaridis beat another future Blue, Maik Taylor, in the Fulham goal from 25 yards to make it 2-2.

FRIDAY 8th AUGUST 1969

Dean Peer was born in Wordsley, Staffordshire. The midfielder was a product of the St Andrew's youth system and made his debut in 1986. Over the next six years Peer made 150 appearances for Blues and scored 12 goals. He was part of the team that won the Leyland-DAF Cup at Wembley in 1991 and helped the club regain Second Division status the following season. After leaving Birmingham the midfielder helped Northampton Town win promotion from the Third Division in 1997.

SATURDAY 9th AUGUST 1969

Defender Garry Pendrey took over the captaincy for the 1969/70 season becoming the youngest skipper in Blues history at the age of 20. A disappointing season started with a 3-1 defeat at Leicester City, and ended with an 18th place finish in Second Division, after Blues had gone winless until mid-September. Phil Summerill scored Blues' goal at Filbert Street, the first of his 13 league goals for the season as he finished top scorer for the second successive season.

FRIDAY 9th AUGUST 1991

Ex-Leeds United and England left-back Terry Cooper was appointed as Blues manager following the departure of Lou Macari. Cooper had enjoyed a trophy-laden career at Elland Road winning the First Division title and FA Cup as well as 20 international caps. After switching to management he won the Fourth Division title with Exeter before landing the job at St Andrew's. Although he guided Blues to the Third Division title in 1992 results tailed off the following season and Barry Fry replaced him in late 1993. Cooper's son Mark also played for City scoring five goals in 44 appearances.

SATURDAY 10th AUGUST 1974

Blues beat Norwich City 3-1 in a Texaco Cup match. Alan Campbell, Bob Hatton and Trevor Francis all scored for City in this Group One game. The Blues finished the group stage of this Anglo-Scottish competition unbeaten after a draw with West Bromwich Albion and Peterborough United. They would make it to the semi-finals of the cup where, for a second year in a row, Newcastle United knocked them out.

SUNDAY 10th AUGUST 1980

Prince Charles was amongst the guests at St Andrew's as the club held its annual open day. The Prince of Wales was given a guided tour of the club's facilities by manager Jim Smith.

MONDAY 11th AUGUST 1975

Jasper Carrott made his first appearance on British television in a BBC Midlands programme about local football called *The Golden Game*. Four years later Carrott would become a director of Birmingham City, a position he held until 1982.

TUESDAY 11th AUGUST 1998

Dele Adebola made it two goals in two games as his strike put Blues on course for a 2-0 League Cup win over Millwall. Michael Johnson scored a late second goal to give City a decisive first-leg advantage. Adebola would top score for Blues during the 1998/99 campaign with 17 goals in all competitions.

SUNDAY 12th AUGUST 1962

Nigel Gleghorn was born in Seaham, County Durham. The former fireman joined Blues from Manchester City for £175,000 in September 1989. He stayed at St Andrew's for three seasons, winning the Football League Trophy in 1991 and top scoring as Blues gained promotion from the Third Division the following year. Gleghorn's 22 goals that season included the winner against Shrewsbury Town, which guaranteed City automatic promotion to the second tier - which had been renamed the First Division following the launch of the Premier League. He scored 43 goals in 176 appearances in all competitions for Birmingham City.

SATURDAY 12th AUGUST 2000

Record signing Geoff Horsfield made his debut in a 0-0 draw with Queens Park Rangers at Loftus Road. Horsfield, who had cost £2.25m when he arrived from Fulham a month earlier, would finish the 2000/2001 season as Blues' top scorer with 12 goals in all competitions. The striker, who was nicknamed 'The Horse', formed an unlikely strike partnership with Christophe Dugarry.

THURSDAY 13th AUGUST 1998

Trevor Francis signed defender Gary Rowett from Derby County for £1m. In an impressive two-year spell with City he clocked up 106 appearances and 12 goals. In both his seasons at the club Blues reached the play-offs and his performances prompted Premier League Leicester City to buy him for £3m in July 2000. Rowett returned to St Andrew's as manager in 2014 and guided a struggling side to Championship survival.

FRIDAY 14th AUGUST 2009

Birmingham City vice-chairman Jack Wiseman died at the age of 92. Wiseman, who was affectionately known as 'Mr Blues', had been a board member of the club since 1956 and had been presented with a lifetime achievement award during the previous season. Blues chairman David Gold said, 'He was Mr Football. One of the greatest sadnesses for me is that Jack in actual fact never received a knighthood for his work in football. Not just for his work for Birmingham City Club but for all he did in the FA. He was so popular and so respected.'

SATURDAY 15th AUGUST 1987

Welsh striker Tony Rees got the new season off to a flying start by scoring Blues' opening goal in just 45 seconds. Rees scored a second shortly after half-time as Stoke City were beaten 2-0.

SATURDAY 15th AUGUST 2009

After a public vote Blues goalkeeping legend Gil Merrick was chosen to represent the club by receiving a plaque on Birmingham's Broad Street Walk of Stars.

SATURDAY 15th AUGUST 2015

Blues goalkeeper Jack Butland became the youngest player to pull on the number one shirt for England when he made his international debut. Butland was aged just 19 years and 158 days when he was selected by England manager Roy Hodgson to start a friendly against Italy.

SUNDAY 16th AUGUST 1998

Birmingham City conceded a goal for the fist time in almost 11 hours of football when Haydn Mullins scored a 73rd minute goal for Crystal Palace. It was the first goal allowed by goalkeeper Ian Bennett and his defence since Gareth Ainsworth had scored for Port Vale the previous April. Bennett had kept clean sheets in the final four matches of the 1997/98 season as well as the opening two games of the new campaign. The defence had held out for 645 minutes when Mullins finally pierced it, but goals from Dele Adebola, Martyn O'Connor and Nicky Forster gave Blues a 3-1 victory.

FRIDAY 17th AUGUST 1956

Birmingham City skipper Len Boyd had his contract terminated at his own request due to a debilitating back problem. The wing-half captained Blues for six years, which included winning the Second Division title in 1955 before finishing 6th and reaching the FA Cup Final a year later. Boyd struggled through the end of that stellar campaign, often having painkilling injections to allow him to play. He played through injury in the cup final and managed only one more Blues appearance, in an Inter-Cities Fairs Cup match against Zagreb, before being forced to retire.

FRIDAY 17th AUGUST 1990

Ian Handysides died in Solihull, aged 27. Over two spells with Birmingham City the midfielder made 133 appearances and scored 12 goals. He was forced to retire in 1988 after being diagnosed with a brain tumour, which two years later had spread to his spine causing his untimely death.

SATURDAY 17th AUGUST 1991

Nigerian international Foley Okenla scored with his first touch in the Football League, as Bury were beaten 3-2 at St Andrew's. Birmingham were leading 2-1 with goals from Nigel Gleghorn and John Gayle when Okenla came on at the break and struck immediately. Despite the bright start to his Blues career Okenla only played six more games and was never offered a contract by City.

SATURDAY 18th AUGUST 1979

Blues wasted a flying start to open the season with a 4-3 home defeat to Fulham. Goals from Tony Evans, who was making his Birmingham City debut, Kevin Dillon and Keith Bertschin, made it a perfect opening 45 minutes for Blues. All the good work was wasted as City conceded four second-half goals to start the campaign with a loss. However, the team turned things around in a season that ended with promotion back to the First Division.

SUNDAY 18th AUGUST 1996

Trevor Francis' reign as Blues manager got off to a winning start with a 1-0 victory over Crystal Palace on the opening day of the season. Winger Paul Devlin got the first goal under the new regime with the winner against the Eagles.

THURSDAY 18th AUGUST 2011

Portuguese side Nacional were the hosts as Birmingham City competed in European football for the first time in nearly 50 years. The two sides met in the play-off round of the Europa League with a place in the group stage at stake. Blues, who had qualified for Europe courtesy of the previous season's League Cup triumph, began their campaign with a goalless draw despite hitting the home woodwork on three occasions.

WEDNESDAY 19th AUGUST 2009

Portsmouth were the first visiting team to play in front of the newly christened Gil Merrick Stand at St Andrew's. The previous April the club had announced that the Railway Stand was to be renamed in honour of the legendary goalkeeper. Fittingly, Blues kept a clean sheet as a last-minute James McFadden penalty secured a 1-0 win.

SATURDAY 20th AUGUST 1938

Birmingham City lost 2-0 to Coventry City in a special friendly to mark the Football League Jubilee. The match was also notable as it was the first time that the team had worn shirts with numbers on the back.

SATURDAY 20th AUGUST 1966

A debut double from winger Bert Murray helped Blues to a 2-1 win at Molineux. Murray had arrived from Chelsea alongside record signing Barry Bridges during the summer. Both players started the game against Wolves with Murray playing a decisive role. He opened the scoring on 52 minutes from Trevor Hockey's cross and doubled Blues' lead 16 minutes later, slamming the ball in from Geoff Vowden's header.

MONDAY 21st AUGUST 1922

Harry Storer took a first class hat-trick as he ripped through the Northamptonshire batting for Derbyshire at Queen's Park in Chesterfield. Storer had already taken two wickets with his leg breaks when he removed opener Claud Woolley for 52. Hamer Bagnall and Lionel Powys-Maurice followed in successive balls as Storer achieved the feat for the only time in his cricketing career.

SATURDAY 21st AUGUST 1965

Blues came out on top as they met Crystal Palace for the first time in the Football League. Outside-left Denis Thwaites scored twice as Birmingham ran out 2-1 winners at St Andrew's.

TUESDAY 22nd AUGUST 1922

Harry Storer took two further wickets to finish with career-best figures of 7-26 as Derbyshire beat Northamptonshire by 53 runs in the County Championship.

SATURDAY 22nd AUGUST 1998

Dele Adebola's hot streak continued as his strike at Bramall Lane made it five goals from five games to start the 1998/99 season. Blues beat Sheffield United thanks to goals from Nicky Forster and Adebola while the home side had Ian Hamilton sent off. The victory maintained a 100% start to the Blues league campaign that would end with Adebola top scoring with 17 goals and the team in third place in the First Division.

SATURDAY 23rd AUGUST 1958

Blues travelled to Villa Park for the season and came away with a point from the Second City derby. Peter Murphy opened the scoring for Birmingham in the first half but future Blue Stan Lynn levelled with a penalty in the second half and the scores finished locked at 1-1.

WEDNESDAY 24th AUGUST 1949

Two goals from Jimmy Dailey earned Blues their first win of the 1949/50 season with a 2-0 victory over West Bromwich Albion. The result proved a false dawn and Birmingham would not win another game until December. Dailey top scored with nine goals as Blues could only manage seven league wins and finished rock bottom of the First Division.

WEDNESDAY 24th AUGUST 1966

Six goals were scored in the last 17 minutes of the match at Fratton Park as Blues edged a nine-goal thriller against Portsmouth. Blues led 2-0 at the break after Geoff Vowden had pounced on a mistake to open the scoring and Barry Bridges had provided a calm finish when put through on the home goal. Brian Lewis pulled a goal back for Portsmouth just before the hour but the floodgates opened in the 73rd minute when Malcolm Beard tucked away a penalty for City. Pompey hit back within 60 seconds through Ray Hiron only for Blues to restore their two-goal lead thanks to Vowden's second. Bert Murray appeared to have made the game safe with an 86th minute strike but two goals in two minutes, from Albert McCann and future Villa boss Tony Barton, pulled it back to 5-4.

SATURDAY 24th AUGUST 1968

Fred Pickering scored after just 13 seconds to set Blues on course for a comprehensive 5-2 victory at Fratton Park. Geoff Vowden doubled the score in the 5th minute and Phil Summerill made it 3-0. Although Portsmouth hit back with two goals, a Johnny Vincent strike and a second goal from Pickering ensured Blues recorded their first win of the season. Pickering and Summerill would end the season with 16 goals each in the league.

SATURDAY 25th AUGUST 1934

Inside-forward Fred Harris scored on his Blues debut to put Birmingham ahead against local rivals Aston Villa. A minute earlier Harris had had an effort disallowed, but he was not to be denied in front of 54,200 at St Andrew's. Joe Bradford was the provider for City's second goal as he set up Bill Guest with a brilliant pass. Villa's Pongo Waring scored a late consolation for the visitors. Over the next 16 years Harris would make over 300 Blues appearances.

WEDNESDAY 25th AUGUST 1965

Former Blue Bryan Orritt denied Birmingham City victory when he scored for Middlesbrough with the final kick of the match. Orritt levelled the scores at 1-1 after Malcolm Beard had put the home side ahead at St Andrew's.

THURSDAY 25th AUGUST 2011

Portuguese side Nacional were comprehensively beaten 3-0 as St Andrew's hosted European football for the first time in nearly half a century. City took control of the tie via Nathan Redmond's superb drive and David Murphy's header from a corner. Chris Wood added a third goal from close range late on to complete the win and ensure progress to the group stage.

SATURDAY 26th AUGUST 1939

Ireland international Jackie Brown was on target as Blues opened the 1939/40 season with a 1-1 draw against Tottenham Hotspur in the Second Division. Birmingham would play two more league games before the outbreak of World War Two caused the suspension of competitive football.

NATHAN REDMOND

TUESDAY 26th AUGUST 2008

Jordon Mutch became the second-youngest player in Blues history when Alex McLeish brought him on at half-time in a League Cup match against Southampton. The midfielder was aged 16 years and 268 days when he entered the fray at St Mary's in a match Blues lost 2-0.

SUNDAY 27th AUGUST 1978

Franck Queudrue was born in Paris, France. The full-back played in Ligue 1 for Lens and the Premier League with Middlesbrough and Fulham before Steve Bruce signed him in a £2.5m deal in 2007. Birmingham were relegated at the end of his first season at the club and Queudrue found himself singled out for criticism from Blues owner David Sullivan. However, he won Player of the Year awards from both fans and local press as the club bounced back to the Premier League the following season while Sullivan made his apologies and sent congratulations. In all the Frenchman played 51 matches for Blues and scored three times.

SATURDAY 27th AUGUST 1983

Birmingham City began the new season with a sponsor's logo across their shirts for the very first time. Brewery Ansells was the first company to pay to emblazon its name across the famous blue shirts. However, the season got off to an inauspicious start with a 4-0 defeat to West Ham United at Upton Park and would end in relegation to the Second Division.

SATURDAY 28th AUGUST 1937

A 2-2 draw with Stoke City set the tone for a season in which Birmingham City would become stalemate specialists. The Welsh duo of Seymour Morris and Dai Richards scored at the Victoria Ground as Blues recorded the first of 18 draws during the 1937/38 campaign.

SATURDAY 28th AUGUST 1965

Centre-half Brian Sharples made Blues history when he became the first Football League substitute used by the club. Sharples replaced Ron Wylie during a 3-3 draw at Preston North End. Geoff Vowden scored Birmingham's opening goal at Deepdale with Malcolm Beard adding goals either side of the break.

THURSDAY 28th AUGUST 1986

Striker Steve Whitton signed for £60,000 from West Ham United following a successful loan spell with Blues. Despite playing in a struggling side Whitton managed 35 goals in 199 matches over three seasons with Birmingham. He was top scorer in 1988 and again the following year before joining Sheffield Wednesday in a £275,000 deal.

WEDNESDAY 29th AUGUST 1956

Alex Govan scored a hat-trick as Birmingham City came out on top in a seven-goal thriller at Fratton Park. It was the first of five hat-tricks that Govan scored during the 1956/57 season. Gordon Astall scored Blues' other goal in the 4-3 victory against Portsmouth.

SATURDAY 29th AUGUST 1964

Stan Lynn scored a penalty for the fifth consecutive match as he got Blues' goal in a 2-1 home defeat to Stoke City. The right-back, who was nicknamed 'Stan the Wham' for his powerful shots and dead ball striking, had scored penalties against Liverpool and Sheffield United in the final two matches of the 1963/64 season. His streak continued with successful spot kicks in the opening three matches of the following season against Nottingham Forest, Fulham and Stoke.

SUNDAY 29th AUGUST 1976

Stephen Carr was born in Dublin, Ireland. The right-back spent 15 years in the top flight of English football with Tottenham Hotspur and Newcastle United before announcing his retirement from football in December 2008. Two months later he joined Blues on a short-term contract and his performances over the next season earned him the captain's armband. Carr became the second Birmingham skipper to lift a major trophy when he led the team to League Cup triumph in 2011.

SATURDAY 30th AUGUST 1969

A quick-fire hat-trick from winger Bert Murray gave Blues a first win of the season as Queens Park Rangers were blown away inside the opening 15 minutes. Murray struck in the 3rd, 5th and 15th minutes to complete his treble and settle this match 3-0 in Birmingham's favour.

WEDNESDAY 30th AUGUST 1972

All three Latchford brothers played in a senior match for the first time as Blues' pair of Dave and Bob faced West Bromwich Albion's Peter. In the event Bob scored past Peter in the Albion goal in the 89th minute to earn Blues a point. Albion had led twice with Bob Hatton pegging them back initially before Latchford made it 2-2.

SUNDAY 30th AUGUST 2009

Karren Brady was revealed as Lord Alan Sugar's new assistant, replacing Margaret Mountford for the sixth series of BBC Television's *The Apprentice*. Brady held the post of managing director at Birmingham for 16 years from March 1993.

TUESDAY 31st AUGUST 1920

Blues got their first win of the Second Division title-winning campaign in style with a 5-1 demolition of Hull City. Johnny Crosbie and Joe Lane scored two goals each for Birmingham City while England international Percy Barton was also on the scoresheet.

WEDNESDAY 31st AUGUST 2011

Just a few hours before the transfer window closed central defender Scott Dann departed for Blackburn Rovers for a fee of £6m, one of the biggest sales in Birmingham City history. Dann had arrived for £3.5m two years earlier after impressing in the Championship with Coventry City and winning England Under-21 caps. Dann's partnership with Roger Johnson was a major factor in the 12-match unbeaten run that helped lay the foundation for a 9th place Premier League finish in 2010. His participation the following season was curtailed by a hamstring injury and that ended his season in January. Dann played 50 Premier League matches for Blues and scored twice.

MONDAY 31st AUGUST 1998

A 17-year-old Andrew Johnson became one of the youngest Blues debutants in club history when he made his bow against Bradford City. Peter Ndlovu scored but City went down 2-1 at Valley Parade. Johnson went on to score 13 goals in 104 appearances for Blues but missed the deciding penalty in the 2001 League Cup final shoot-out.

BIRMINGHAM CITY
On This Day

SEPTEMBER

SATURDAY 1st SEPTEMBER 1894

Small Heath met local rivals Aston Villa in a league match for the first time. Blues travelled the short distance to Wellington Road for a First Division clash, which they lost 2-1. Tommy Hands scored Small Heath's goal in front of a crowd of 20,000.

TUESDAY 1st SEPTEMBER 1942

Terry Hennessey was born in Llay, Wales. The defensive midfielder signed with Birmingham City as a junior and made his debut in 1961. He went on to make over 200 appearances for Blues, scoring three goals, and was a member of the 1963 League Cup-winning team. Hennessey made his debut for Wales in 1962 and went on to win 39 caps.

FRIDAY 1st SEPTEMBER 1995

Blues signed Notts County central defender Michael Johnson for a fee of £225,000. Johnson's performances and aerial ability earned him the nickname 'Magic' – in reference to American basketball legend Earvin 'Magic' Johnson – from the St Andrew's faithful. He was a key part of the team that reached four successive league play-offs and finished runners-up in the 2001 League Cup. Johnson made over 300 appearances for Blues and scored 17 goals.

WEDNESDAY 2nd SEPTEMBER 1953

Centre forward Ted Purdon opened the scoring against Plymouth Argyle in just 15 seconds. It was one of the fastest strikes in club history and set Blues on course for a comfortable 3-0 win. Noel Kinsey scored Blues' second goal against the Pilgrims with Jackie Stewart adding a third.

SATURDAY 3rd SEPTEMBER 1892

Small Heath hosted Burslem Port Vale at Muntz Street for the club's first ever Football League fixture. The visitors arrived late and short of their centre-forward – who had missed the team's train – and were no match for Blues. Freddie Wheldon scored the team's first goal in the new league and George Scott added a second. Wheldon made it three before Jack Hallam's 20-yard rocket and Harry Edwards' breakaway goal completed a one-sided 5-1 victory in front of 2,500 spectators.

SATURDAY 3rd SEPTEMBER 1994

Striker Dave Regis scored twice to set up a 4-2 win over Plymouth Argyle, which kick-started a 20-match unbeaten run for Blues. Former Manchester United winger Danny Wallace scored his second and final Blues goal while Paul Tait was also on target. Blues remained unbeaten until the following January setting a club record in the process and putting Barry Fry's side on course for the Second Division title.

WEDNESDAY 4th SEPTEMBER 1929

Joe Bradford hit his ninth Birmingham City hat-trick as West Ham United were beaten 4-2 in a First Division match at St Andrew's.

MONDAY 4th SEPTEMBER 1967

Five different Blues players found the target as Hull City were hit for six at St Andrew's. Fred Pickering scored his first goal since arriving in a £55,000 deal from Everton. Barry Bridges, who would finish the season as the club's top scorer with 28, opened the scoring with a close-range header and added a third after Bert Murray's thunderbolt had doubled the lead. Geoff Vowden and Johnny Vincent scored Blues' other goals in a 6-2 win.

SATURDAY 4th SEPTEMBER 1971

Maik Taylor was born in Hildesheim, West Germany. Blues boss Steve Bruce originally signed the goalkeeper in August 2003 from Fulham, on a loan deal. Taylor's performances earned him a £1.5m permanent move to St Andrew's the following March. He appeared 210 times for Blues and earned 55 Northern Ireland caps while at Birmingham City, which is a club record. However, he found competition with England goalkeepers Joe Hart and Ben Foster limited his opportunities and moved to Leeds United after his contract expired in 2011.

SATURDAY 5th SEPTEMBER 1970

Boy wonder Trevor Francis made his Blues debut coming on as a second half for Bob Latchford at Ninian Park in a 2-0 defeat to Cardiff City. Francis was just 16 years and 139 days old and he remains the youngest ever player to have represented Birmingham City in a competitive fixture.

MONDAY 5th SEPTEMBER 1977

After losing the first five matches of the season the Birmingham City board informed Blues manager Willie Bell that his contract would not be renewed. Bell had staved off relegation in his first season in charge of the club and improved to 13th place in his second campaign. He had also overseen the signings of Keith Bertschin, Gary Jones and Jim Montgomery. However, he had lost almost half of his 88 games in charge of the team and a winless start to the season cost him his job.

THURSDAY 5th SEPTEMBER 1991

Blues manager Terry Cooper signed his son Mark Cooper from his former club Exeter City. The midfielder played a total of 44 games, and scored five goals for Birmingham City before leaving for Fulham in a £40,000 deal in November 1992.

TUESDAY 5th SEPTEMBER 2000

A 0-0 draw with Southend United at Roots Hall made sure Blues cleared the first hurdle on the way to the League Cup final in Cardiff. Birmingham had gone into this second leg match with a comfortable advantage from the first match at St Andrew's. A goal each from Nicky Eaden, Michael Johnson, Dele Adebola, Marcelo and Bryan Hughes had given City a 5-0 win in the first leg.

SATURDAY 6th SEPTEMBER 1980

Champions Liverpool visited St Andrew's and were held to a 1-1 draw by Birmingham City. Frank Worthington's goal earned Blues a point as he levelled the match just four minutes after Kenny Dalglish had given the visitors the lead.

SATURDAY 7th SEPTEMBER 1889

Small Heath made a winning start in the Football Alliance with a 3-2 victory over Birmingham St Georges. Forwards Charlie Short, Eddy Stanley and Will Devey shared Blues' goals. The Football Alliance ran for three seasons before merging with the Football League to create the Second Division. Blues finished 10th in the first two seasons but improved to take third place in the final edition of the Alliance.

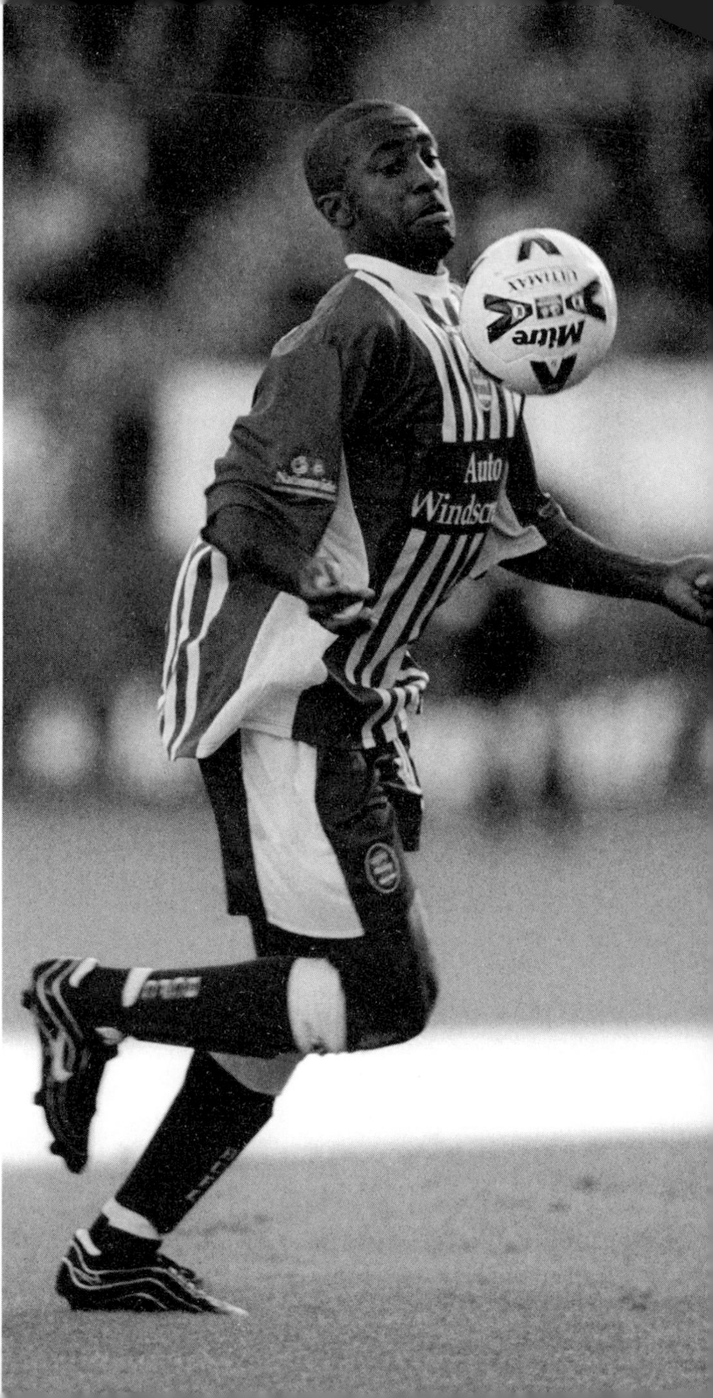

MICHAEL JOHNSON

SATURDAY 7th SEPTEMBER 1895

Small Heath goalkeeper Jim Roach suffered a nightmare opening 45 minutes on his debut. Aston Villa scored five first-half goals at Wellington Road, although the *Birmingham Daily Post*, said Roach's struggles were due to having the sun in his eyes. Small Heath did recover after the break winning the second half 3-2 with goals from Billy Walton, Frank Mobley and Tommy Hands. The final score was 7-3 to the hosts, which is the highest aggregate score for a Second City derby.

SATURDAY 7th SEPTEMBER 1968

Blues striker Geoff Vowden became the first substitute in the history of the Football League to score a hat-trick. Blues were two goals up against Huddersfield Town when Vowden was brought on for Ron Wylie in the 50th minute. Future Birmingham City striker Frank Worthington pulled a goal back for the Terriers but after that it was all Vowden. The striker scored two headers in three minutes to kill off any hopes the visitors had of mounting a comeback before sealing a 5-1 win by pouncing on a goalkeeping error in the 89th minute.

FRIDAY 8th SEPTEMBER 1854

Billy Edmunds was born in Bordesley Green, Birmingham. In 1877 Edmunds was appointed as Small Heath's first official captain. He had played in the club's first matches two years earlier and was a fixture in the side for a decade. As captain the half-back led Small Heath on a 22-match unbeaten run and after retiring from playing he was appointed as the club's first honorary secretary.

SATURDAY 8th SEPTEMBER 1894

'Diamond' Freddie Wheldon missed the first ever penalty kick awarded to Small Heath. The striker made amends by scoring both goals in a 2-0 win against Bolton Wanderers. The penalty kick had been introduced to league football three years earlier.

SATURDAY 8th SEPTEMBER 1956

Scottish outside-left Alex Govan hit his third hat-trick in 11 days as he got all the goals in a 3-0 victory over Preston North End.

THURSDAY 8th SEPTEMBER 1977

Blues appointed Sir Alf Ramsey, the man who had guided England to World Cup glory in 1966, as the club's manager following the dismissal of Willie Bell. Ramsey, who was a Birmingham City director, became the first knight of the realm to manage a Football League club, but his reign only lasted seven months before poor health forced him to step down.

WEDNESDAY 9th SEPTEMBER 1953

Inside-left Peter Murphy smashed a nine-minute hat-trick, as Luton Town were thrashed 5-1. Murphy's treble is one of the fastest hat-tricks in Blues history. South African-born Ted Purdon scored City's other goals in this Second Division victory.

SATURDAY 10th SEPTEMBER 1892

Small Heath visited Walsall Town Swifts' new home at The Chuckery for the first ever Football League meeting between the two sides and came away with a comfortable 3-1 victory. Goals from 'Diamond' Freddie Wheldon and Caesar Jenkyns, as well as an Alf Pinches own goal, gave the visitors the points.

TUESDAY 11th SEPTEMBER 1877

Small Heath Alliance played at Muntz Street for the first time beating Saltley College 5-0 in a friendly match. It was the start of a 22-match unbeaten run that began life at the ground. The ground, which was known as Coventry Road while in use by Small Heath, had few facilities when it opened. However, the club built one stand and bought another stand from Aston Villa's Wellington Road ground for £90 to give the stadium a capacity of 30,000.

WEDNESDAY 11th SEPTEMBER 1946

John Roberts was born in Abercynon, Wales. Blues manager Freddie Goodwin broke the club transfer record when he brought the defender to the club for £140,000 in 1972. It was the first time that Birmingham had spent a six-figure sum on any player and Goodwin claimed, 'It was money well spent.' Roberts, who was a Welsh international, had won a championship medal as part of Arsenal's double winning side in 1971. In four seasons he played in 79 Blues matches and scored one goal.

SATURDAY 12th SEPTEMBER 1970

Trevor Francis scored the first of his 133 Blues goals to give City the lead against Oxford United at St Andrew's. Birmingham were held to a 1-1 draw after Roy Clayton cancelled out Francis' opener while Bob Latchford had a goal ruled out.

SATURDAY 12th SEPTEMBER 1998

Birmingham City's first visit to Bolton Wanderers' Reebok Stadium got off to the worst possible start when Trotters striker Bob Taylor scored after just 18 seconds. Things went from bad to worse for Blues as Per Frandsen doubled the home lead in the 5th minute. Gary Rowett pulled a goal back shortly before the break but Taylor's second goal made the final score 3-1 to the home side.

SATURDAY 13th SEPTEMBER 1902

The first home match of the 1902/03 season resulted in a comfortable 4-0 win for Small Heath over visitors Manchester City. Irish inside-forward Arthur Leonard scored twice in the match and would go on to add another 14 in the league making him Blues' top marksman for the campaign. Forwards Bob McRoberts and Billy Jones scored a goal apiece as Blues began a season that would end with a 100% home record and promotion to the First Division.

THURSDAY 13th SEPTEMBER 1990

Kevin Ashley became the most expensive player to depart St Andrew's since the sale of Trevor Francis over a decade earlier. The Kings Heath-born defender moved to Wolverhampton Wanderers in a £500,000 deal. Ashley had progressed through the youth system at Birmingham City making his debut in 1987. He made 67 appearances in all competitions and scored one goal before moving to Molineux.

TUESDAY 13th SEPTEMBER 1994

Gary Bull scored on his Birmingham City debut to earn Blues a 1-1 draw with Rotherham United. Bull scored six more goals in a successful spell on loan from Nottingham Forest. He returned on a permanent deal the following year but only scored one more goal before leaving for York City.

SATURDAY 14th SEPTEMBER 1901

Small Heath went to the summit of the First Division after beating Manchester City 4-1 at Hyde Road. Jack Aston scored twice while Bob McRoberts and Johnny McMillan got one apiece as Blues made it five points from the first three games of the season. However, the team's early form proved deceptive and a poor season ended with relegation.

SATURDAY 14th SEPTEMBER 1918

England international and future national captain Jesse Pennington featured as a guest player for Blues, when they went down 3-2 to Nottingham Forest in a Midland League wartime match. The left-back, who was known as 'Peerless' Pennington, went on to win a championship medal with West Bromwich Albion in 1920. Jackie Whitehouse and Billy Walker scored Blues' goals against Forest.

SATURDAY 14th SEPTEMBER 1974

Blues held off a late Derby County charge despite being reduced to 10 men by Howard Kendall's injury. Bob Hatton had given Birmingham a 1-0 lead at half-time with his first goal of the season. After the break Joe Gallagher's pressure at a corner led to a handball in the visitors' penalty area and Trevor Francis converted the spot kick. Following the loss of Kendall the Rams were in the ascendancy, but Blues increased their lead further as Francis won, and scored, a second penalty. Late goals from Roger Davies and Bruce Rioch ensured a nervy ending but Blues held on for a 3-2 win.

THURSDAY 15th SEPTEMBER 2011

Blues' hopes of progressing in the Europa League suffered a major blow as they were outclassed by Braga. The Portuguese side, who had finished runners up in the competition the previous season, ran out 3-1 winners at St Andrew's thanks to Jorge Helder Barbosa's double strike and a Lima goal, while Marlon King converted a close range chance for Blues. Birmingham boss Chris Hughton said, 'I've no arguments with the result. What we saw in Braga was a team who once they got into the forward areas and close to goal, they were more clinical and showed better quality than we did.'

SATURDAY 16th SEPTEMBER 1893

Small Heath set the club record with a 13th consecutive victory. Walsall Town Swifts were beaten 4-0 at Muntz Street to set the record with Stourbridge-born Charlie Izon scoring a hat-trick on his debut, a feat that has only been equalled once since. Welsh centre-half Caesar Jenkyns scored Blues' other goal against Walsall.

SATURDAY 16th SEPTEMBER 1905

Blues recorded a league victory over local rivals Aston Villa for the first time, with a 2-0 win in front of 30,000 spectators at Muntz Street. Forwards Billy Jones and Arthur Mounteney were the Birmingham scorers in a famous win.

MONDAY 16th SEPTEMBER 2002

The first Second City derby to take place in the Premier League era ended in a comprehensive 3-0 victory for Blues. Clinton Morrison gave the home side a first-half lead with a close range finish before Villa collapsed in the second half. The visitors' goalkeeper Peter Enckelman gifted Blues a second goal when he missed a simple clearance and had to watch as the ball rolled into the net. Sub Geoff Horsfield completed the win by robbing Turkish defender Alpay of the ball before rifling it past Enckelman.

SATURDAY 17th SEPTEMBER 1892

Sheffield United inflicted the first defeat on Blues since they joined the Football League as they went down 2-0 at Bramall Lane.

WEDNESDAY 17th SEPTEMBER 1958

Blues centre forward Eddie Brown scored all four goals as Leeds United were crushed 4-1 at St Andrew's. The visitors took an early lead but Brown levelled from close range after taking Gordon Astall's pass. He hit a second goal before half-time with a low shot into the bottom corner. Brown got his hat-trick with a ball that cannoned in off the crossbar, with the linesman confirming it had crossed the goal-line. He completed the scoring in the 69th minute to become the first Blues player to score four in a game since Jackie Stewart a decade earlier.

TUESDAY 17th SEPTEMBER 1974

Kenny Burns scored twice as Ayr United were brushed aside 3-0 in the Texaco Cup. Jimmy Calderwood scored Blues' third goal and a goalless second leg in Scotland ensured progress in the competition.

SATURDAY 18th SEPTEMBER 1926

Roy Warhurst was born in Sheffield, South Yorkshire. Blues manager Bob Brocklebank brought the Sheffield United winger to St Andrew's in 1950 in an £8,000 deal and converted him into a wing-half. Warhurst became an integral part of the club's success under Arthur Turner helping Birmingham win the Second Division title and reach Wembley a year later. However, he was forced to miss the FA Cup Final with a thigh injury and City winger Alex Govan claimed that 'If Roy Warhurst had been fit then there would only have been one winner.' The following season Warhurst took over the captaincy from Len Boyd before moving to Manchester City for £10,000 in 1957.

TUESDAY 18th SEPTEMBER 1990

Dennis Bailey scored as Blues were held to a 1-1 draw by Exeter City. It was the first of eight consecutive draws for Blues.

WEDNESDAY 19th SEPTEMBER 1973

Blues visited the Victoria Ground for their first ever Texaco Cup fixture which ended 0-0 against Stoke City.

TUESDAY 19th SEPTEMBER 2000

Andrew Johnson's 87th minute winner gave Blues a narrow 4-3 advantage after a rollercoaster League Cup tie against Wycombe Wanderers. Birmingham appeared to have thrown the game away as the home side came back from 3-0 down to level the contest at Adams Park. City had come hurtling out of the blocks with three goals in the opening 25 minutes thanks to a Paul McCarthy own goal as well as goals from Geoff Horsfield and Johnson. Andy Rammell gave the home side hope on the stroke of half-time and sub Andy Baird scored with his first touch to reduce the deficit further. Then Jamie Bates appeared to have salvaged a draw for Wycombe but Johnson had the final word.

THURSDAY 19th SEPTEMBER 2013

Jesse Lingard arrived on loan from Manchester United. The 20-year-old made his Birmingham debut 48 hours later and enjoyed a dream start to life at St Andrew's. He scored a hat-trick in the first half against Sheffield Wednesday and he added a fourth after the interval for good measure as Blues ran out 4-1 victors.

SATURDAY 20th SEPTEMBER 1975

Willie Bell's reign as Blues manager got off to a flying start as Burnley were brushed aside 4-0 at St Andrew's. The visitors put up stubborn resistance in the first half and some determined defending kept the match scoreless at the interval. Blues cut loose in the second half with Alan Campbell, Peter Withe, Howard Kendall and Trevor Francis all on target.

TUESDAY 20th SEPTEMBER 1988

Blues' first league meeting with Walsall in over 85 years ended in a catastrophic 5-0 defeat at Fellows Park. The result remains Birmingham's worst loss to the Saddlers.

SATURDAY 21st SEPTEMBER 1968

Blues romped to their biggest ever win over local rivals Aston Villa with a 4-0 triumph at St Andrew's. Geoff Vowden, Jimmy Greenhoff, Johnny Vincent and Phil Summerill scored City's goals in the match.

SATURDAY 21st SEPTEMBER 1996

The antics of Manchester City's Uwe Rosler and the award of a harsh 88th minute penalty combined to push Blues right-back Gary Poole over the edge at Maine Road. Rosler's play-acting won a free kick at Poole's expense and from the dead ball the spot kick was awarded for handball against Paul Furlong. The two decisions were too much for Poole to take and he responded by shoving referee Richard Poulain. He received his marching orders for his actions while Georgi Kinkladze dispatched the penalty kick to make it 1-0. Poole received a four-match ban and was sold by manager Trevor Francis the following month to Charlton Athletic for £250,000.

TUESDAY 21st SEPTEMBER 2010

Czech defender Martin Jiranek made his debut as Blues brushed aside MK Dons on their way to the League Cup final at Wembley. Three goals in four first-half minutes ended the third round tie as a contest. Alexander Hleb, Nikola Zigic and Craig Gardner were all on target as Birmingham City won 3-1.

SATURDAY 22nd SEPTEMBER 1900

Gainsborough Trinity were thrashed 6-0 in a Second Division match at Muntz Street. Top scorer Bob McRoberts and centre-half Alex Leake scored two goals each against Trinity, with Billy Walton and a John Thornley own goal completing the scoring.

TUESDAY 22nd SEPTEMBER 1998

Zimbabwe international striker Peter Ndlovu scored two early goals to set Blues on their way to a 6-0 victory over Macclesfield Town in the League Cup. Chris Marsden, Gary Rowett, Michael Johnson and a John Askey own goal completed the scoring for City. The score equalled Blues' biggest victory in a League Cup match and completed a 9-0 aggregate win as the team strolled past the Silkmen and into the next round.

MONDAY 22nd SEPTEMBER 2014

Former Birmingham City managing director Karren Brady was elevated to the House of Lords as a Conservative life peer when she was created Baroness Brady of Knightsbridge.

SATURDAY 23rd SEPTEMBER 1893

A Caesar Jenkyns goal could not prevent Small Heath from going down 3-1 to Liverpool at Anfield. The result was the club's first defeat in 14 matches.

MONDAY 23rd SEPTEMBER 1968

Liam Daish was born in Portsmouth, Hampshire. Barry Fry signed the defender from Cambridge United for a fee of £50,000 in January 1994. Daish was at St Andrew's for just over two years scoring six goals in 98 first team outings. He was captain of the side that secured the lower league double of the Second Division title and Football League Trophy in 1995.

MONDAY 24th SEPTEMBER 1984

Everton manager Howard Kendall paid Blues £100,000 to secure the services of Pat Van Den Hauwe. The defender joined Birmingham as an apprentice in 1976 making his debut two years later. He was ever-present during the 1983/84 season but became a transfer target following the club's relegation. At Everton Van Den Hauwe went on to win two league titles and a European Cup Winners' Cup as well as Wales caps.

FRIDAY 25th SEPTEMBER 1925

Fred Slater was born in Burton upon Trent, Staffordshire. The centre-forward joined Blues in 1947 but had to wait a year for his first taste of first team action. He made his debut in November 1948 in a home game against Huddersfield Town and suffered a broken leg that kept him out for four months. Slater only played four more games for Birmingham before joining York City.

WEDNESDAY 26th SEPTEMBER 1962

Birmingham City's successful League Cup run got off to a flying start as Doncaster Rovers were hammered 5-0 in the second round at St Andrew's. Ken Leek scored twice for Blues with Jimmy Bloomfield, Jimmy Harris and Bertie Auld all contributing a goal to the victory.

SATURDAY 27th SEPTEMBER 1879

A local rivalry was born as Small Heath took on Aston Villa for the very first time. The first meeting between the two clubs took place on waterlogged Muntz Street pitch with the hosts winning by a goal and 'a disputed goal' to nil.

WEDNESDAY 27th SEPTEMBER 1961

The first leg of the Inter-Cities Fairs Cup final against Italian giants Roma finished all square after Blues staged a late comeback at St Andrew's. Roma's Argentine centre-forward Pedro Manfredini scored twice to put the visitors in command. Mike Hellawell gave the Blues hope with a shot that surprised Roma keeper Fabio Cudicini and with time running out Bryan Orritt forced the ball home from a goalmouth scramble to make the final score 2-2.

SATURDAY 28th SEPTEMBER 1929

Joe Bradford's second hat-trick in successive matches, and third during the month, was not enough to prevent a 7-5 defeat to Blackburn Rovers at Ewood Park. On this occasion Bradford was outshone by Blackburn's Syd Puddefoot who scored four for the home side, while Johnny Crosbie chipped in with the other two Blues goals.

SATURDAY 28th SEPTEMBER 1985

A 3-1 defeat to Queens Park Rangers was the start of an eight-match losing run that equalled the worst sequence in the club's history. Ken Armstrong scored Blues' goal at Loftus Road.

THURSDAY 29th SEPTEMBER 2011

Wade Elliott's late strike sealed a comeback win and earned Birmingham City a first victory in the group stage of the Europa League. Blues had fallen behind to Slovenian club NK Maribor after goalkeeper Colin Doyle had missed Jonathan Spector's back pass allowing Dalibor Volas a simple tap-in. But City fought back with Chris Burke levelling matters from Marlon King's reverse pass. And then Elliott scored with a 25-yard strike as Maribor goalkeeper Jasmin Handanovic allowed the ball to squirm through him and into the net.

WEDNESDAY 30th SEPTEMBER 1964

Goals from Stan Lynn and Ken Leek secured a 2-0 win over struggling Wolverhampton Wanderers at Molineux. Lynn gave Blues the lead as he slammed home a shot from close range after the referee awarded an indirect free kick rather than a penalty when Alec Jackson was fouled inside the home area. Leek doubled City's lead with a long-range shot after 40 minutes.

SATURDAY 30th SEPTEMBER 1978

Blues goalkeeper Jim Montgomery made his 600th senior appearance as the team visited Elland Road. Over 500 of Montgomery's appearance were for Sunderland and he is best remembered for his performance in the 1973 FA Cup Final where he denied Leeds United with a string of incredible saves. The stopper could not repeat the trick against the Yorkshiremen on this occasion and the home side ran out 3-0 winners.

BIRMINGHAM CITY
On This Day

OCTOBER

SATURDAY 1st OCTOBER 1938

The day after announcing we have 'Peace for our Time' Neville Chamberlain was the guest of honour at The Valley to see Charlton Athletic take on Blues. The Prime Minister made the statement following his infamous meeting with German Chancellor Adolf Hitler in Munich. In London the Blues rallied after being hit with a Jonathan Wilkinson hat-trick inside the opening half an hour. Two goals from Fred Harris in addition to one each from Ted Duckhouse and Frank White earned Blues a 4-4 draw.

SATURDAY 1st OCTOBER 1955

Scottish winger Alex Govan created all three goals as Birmingham City swept aside a struggling Tottenham Hotspur side at St Andrew's. Blues went 1-0 up after Govan got the better of Danny Blanchflower and put in an awkward cross that Harry Clarke could only head into his own net. The home side continued to dominate but could not extend their lead until late in the game. With 15 minutes left Govan supplied the cross for Eddie Brown to head a second goal and the Scot teed up Peter Murphy for a last-minute tap-in to make it 3-0.

SATURDAY 2nd OCTOBER 1920

After a slow start to the season Birmingham City's campaign clicked into gear with a 5-0 thrashing of Leicester City. Joe Lane scored a hat-trick with Harry Hampton scoring his first two goals of the season. Hampton ended the season as top scorer with 16 as the team won the Second Division title.

SATURDAY 2nd OCTOBER 1976

Blues striker Kenny Burns scored four goals as Derby County were swept aside 5-1. John Connolly got Blues' other goal at St Andrew's as a depleted Derby team were put to the sword. Burns' four goals took his tally to seven for the season and he would end with 20 in all competitions. Burns started life at St Andrew's as a defender but was moved forward following the departure of Bob Latchford. In seven years at City he scored 53 goals in 204 appearances before being sold to Nottingham Forest where he returned to defence.

SATURDAY 3rd OCTOBER 1959

Legendary Blues goalkeeper Gil Merrick marked his record 551st, and final, match, between the posts with a clean sheet against Leeds United. The First Division match at St Andrew's ended 2-0 to Blues with Jim Barrett and Brian Taylor scoring the home goals.

SATURDAY 4th OCTOBER 1890

Hednesford Town were thrashed 8-0 in the first qualifying round of the FA Cup. 'Diamond' Freddie Wheldon led the rout with a hat-trick with Will Devey adding two while Jack Hallam, Caesar Jenkyns and an own goal completed the scoring. In the Small Heath team was Charlie Short, who had not been registered properly, an oversight that led to the club's disqualification from the FA Cup for the 1890/91 season.

SATURDAY 5th OCTOBER 1968

Striker Jimmy Greenhoff scored four goals as Blues edged out Fulham in a nine-goal thriller at St Andrew's. Midfielder Johnny Vincent opened the scoring after just two minutes and Greenhoff added two more as Birmingham reached the break 3-0 up. However, three Fulham goals in eight minutes after the restart turned the match on its head. Greenhoff completed his hat-trick and although Fulham levelled again he then got a fourth to make the final score 5-4.

SATURDAY 6th OCTOBER 1894

Small Heath rallied from a 3-0 half-time deficit to overcome Wolverhampton Wanderers 4-3 in a First Division clash at Muntz Street. Inside-forward Billy Walton scored twice while Freddie Wheldon and Frank Mobley got a goal apiece to complete a remarkable comeback.

SATURDAY 6th OCTOBER 1945

Blues recorded their biggest victory during the wartime leagues of World War Two with an 8-0 thrashing of Tottenham Hotspur at St Andrew's. Defender Ted Duckhouse got the ball rolling against hapless Spurs with a spectacular 50-yard shot. Centre forward Dave Massart added another two as did outside-right Jock Mulraney. Neil Dougall, Harold Bodle and Welsh international George Edwards all scored a goal apiece for City in the rout.

TUESDAY 6th OCTOBER 2009

Carson Yeung's Grandtop International Holdings completed its protracted takeover of Birmingham City. Yeung had first made an abortive attempt to buy the club two years earlier, acquiring 29.9% of the club's shares but failing to find the necessary funds to complete the deal before a deadline. He returned in August 2009 with another offer for Birmingham City and the £81.5m deal was completed two months later. Following completion of the deal Grandtop re-registered the club as a private company and renamed the holding company Birmingham International Holdings.

WEDNESDAY 7th OCTOBER 1959

Birmingham City took a useful lead in the Inter-Cities Fairs Cup semi-final against Belgian side Union Saint-Gilloise. Blues trailed to an early goal in Brussels but rallied before half-time through Harry Hooper and Johnny Gordon strikes. The hosts scored one minute after the restart but further goals from Brian Taylor and James Barrett gave Blues a commanding 4-2 lead at the end of the first leg.

SATURDAY 7th OCTOBER 1967

A Barry Bridges double at Villa Park put Blues on course for victory in the first Second City derby to be played as a Second Division fixture. A crowd of 49,984 witnessed a 4-2 Birmingham win with further strikes coming from Geoff Vowden and a Malcolm Beard penalty.

SATURDAY 8th OCTOBER 1932

Outside-left Jack Thorogood scored his second goal in as many matches, as Sheffield Wednesday were beaten 2-1 in the First Division. Unfortunately Thorogood's hot streak did not continue and the two goals he scored during October 1932 were the only two of his four-year Blues career. Inside-right Tom Grosvenor scored City's other goal against the Owls in front of 14,999 at St Andrew's.

SATURDAY 9th OCTOBER 1965

A goal from inside-forward Alec Jackson gave Blues victory in their first league meeting with Norwich City. Jackson's 17th minute strike secured a 1-0 win in front of 11,622 at St Andrew's in a Second Division clash.

SUNDAY 10th OCTOBER 1971

Ian Bennett was born in Worksop, Nottingham. Blues manager Barry Fry signed Bennett from Peterborough United for a £325,000 fee in December 1993. The goalkeeper was ever-present in the team that won the Second Division title and Football League Trophy in 1995. In 12 years at St Andrew's Bennett clocked up over 350 appearances for Blues across three divisions of English football. He was outstanding in the 2001 League Cup final making several top-class saves and denying Dietmar Hamann in the penalty shoot-out.

WEDNESDAY 11th OCTOBER 1961

Blues went down 2-0 in a bad-tempered second leg of the Inter-Cities Fairs Cup final at the Stadio Olimpico in Rome. Roma's players resorted to body checks and other dirty tricks while manager Luis Carniglia repeatedly came onto the pitch. The City players were also pelted with sand by the home support in Rome. An unfortunate Brian Farmer own goal and a long distance Paolo Pestrin strike in the last minute gave the Italians victory. Blues manager Gil Merrick said, 'Roma were the better footballing side and deserved to win. But they did not show any sportsmanship.'

SATURDAY 12th OCTOBER 1974

Blues legend Trevor Francis scored his first top-flight hat-trick with all three goals in a 3-0 victory against Luton Town. The forward would score two more Birmingham hat-tricks on his way to a total of 133 City goals.

SUNDAY 12th OCTOBER 1997

Midfielder Chris Marsden took just eight minutes to endear himself to Blues fans by scoring the winner on his debut against his former club Wolverhampton Wanderers. Marsden had arrived from Stockport County 48 hours earlier in a £500,000 deal and marked his first appearance with the only goal in a 1-0 win.

SATURDAY 13th OCTOBER 1906

Blues goalkeeper Nat Robinson missed the match at Sheffield United after making 121 consecutive appearances for the team. Jack Dorrington deputised for Robinson but could not prevent the team from losing 2-0 at Bramall Lane.

SATURDAY 13th OCTOBER 1956

Inside-forward Bunny Larkin scored on his debut to earn Blues a point in a 1-1 draw with Leeds United at Elland Road. Larkin would go on to score 29 goals in 92 Blues matches before transferring to Norwich City. He was Birmingham City's top scorer during the 1958/59 season with 23 goals, including four in the Inter-Cities Fairs Cup. Larkin said, 'I'd always scored goals wherever I'd played. I had the advantage of being able to use both feet to shoot. That meant that you didn't have to change your position when the ball came to you. There don't seem to be many players around nowadays that can do that.'

SATURDAY 14th OCTOBER 1893

Centre-half Caesar Jenkyns was the first Small Heath player ever sent off after he pushed over Liverpool's Joe McQue. Jenkyns sought retribution after McQue had kicked Frank Mobley, but was dismissed for his actions. Liverpool took advantage of their extra man with a last minute goal to win the match 4-3. Before leaving the field Jenkyns had found the target for Small Heath with Freddie Wheldon and Tommy Hands scoring the home side's other goals at Muntz Street.

TUESDAY 14th OCTOBER 1958

Birmingham City drew 2-2 in Germany in an Inter-Cities Fairs Cup tie with the Cologne XI. Blues came from two goals down to level through Dick Neal and Harry Hooper at the Mungersdorfer Stadion in Cologne.

MONDAY 15th OCTOBER 2001

Blues manager Trevor Francis left the club by mutual consent. Under Francis the team had made the Championship play-offs in three successive seasons but failed to reach the final on each occasion, twice going out via a penalty shoot-out. He had also led Blues to the 2001 League Cup final only to suffer penalty heartbreak once more. A poor start to the season had seen City's promotion bid falter and even though victory over Barnsley halted a six-match losing streak Francis departed St Andrew's. In total Francis was in charge for 290 matches, which is a club record.

SATURDAY 16th OCTOBER 1954

Centre forward Eddie Brown made his Blues debut against Swansea Town after joining in a £9,000 deal earlier in the month. Brown completed Blues' famous 1950s forward line along with Peter Murphy, Noel Kinsey and Alex Govan. Over the next couple of seasons the quartet's goals would fire Birmingham to promotion, a 6th place top-flight finish and the FA Cup Final. Brown's contribution in that time was 90 goals in 185 appearances for City. Murphy was on target twice against Swansea as Blues ran out 2-0 winners.

THURSDAY 16th OCTOBER 2014

Blues legend Trevor Francis was inducted into the English Hall of Fame at the National Football Museum in Manchester. The former Birmingham City player and manager was chosen by a panel, which included Sir Bobby Charlton and Sir Alex Ferguson.

MONDAY 17th OCTOBER 1881

Small Heath beat Derby Town 4-1 in the first round of the FA Cup. It was Blues' first ever FA Cup tie and centre-forward Billy Slater had the honour of scoring their first goal in the competition. Slater scored a second goal against Derby with further strikes coming from Walter Hands and Arthur Jones ensured Small Heath progressed to the next round.

SATURDAY 17th OCTOBER 1925

Blues staged a remarkable late rally to earn a point in the Second City derby at Villa Park. The home side were leading 3-0 with just 11 minutes left on the clock and things were looking bleak for the visitors. However, a brace from top scorer Joe Bradford gave Blues hope before Villa keeper Cyril Spiers put the goal into his own net to level the scores at 3-3.

MONDAY 17th OCTOBER 2016

Trillion Trophy Asia, the investment vehicle of Chinese businessman Paul Suen Cho Hung, completed its purchase of a majority stake in Birmingham International Holdings (BIH). It was the end of a process that saw BIH restructured, relisted and taken out of voluntary receivership.

SATURDAY 18th OCTOBER 1986

Blues ended an eight-match winless streak in style with a 4-1 victory over high-flying Crystal Palace in the Second Division. Striker Steve Whitton scored the pick of the Birmingham goals with a 30-yard rocket, which came from a well-worked free kick move after a foul on Andy Kennedy. Des Bremner and Vince Overson had given Blues a two-goal advantage in the first half. City's Wayne Clarke rounded off the scoring in the final minute of the game.

WEDNESDAY 19th OCTOBER 1960

Birmingham City opened their Inter-Cities Fairs Cup campaign for 1960/61 with a hard-fought 3-2 victory over Budapest side Ujpesti Dozsa. The Hungarians twice took the lead at St Andrew's with both goals scored by their international striker Janos Gorocs. Johnny Gordon hit both the first equaliser and a late winner while Gordon Astall levelled the scores a second time.

SATURDAY 19th OCTOBER 1985

Midfielder Lee Jenkins suffered a nightmare debut at The Hawthorns as he sustained a broken leg that ended his Blues career. The former Villa player did recover from the injury but never played another game for City and was given a free transfer at the end of the 1985/86 season and moved to Finland where he joined FinnPa. Birmingham went down 2-1 to West Bromwich Albion despite taking an early lead through Scottish striker Andy Kennedy.

TUESDAY 19th OCTOBER 2010

Blues rode their luck against Brentford to scrape through to the fifth round of the League Cup. The Bees had already knocked Everton and looked like they might take another Premier League scalp when Sam Wood volleyed them into the lead. Blues wasted several good chances to level the match before Kevin Phillips finally beat Brentford keeper Richard Lee with a low shot in the 92nd minute. Extra time could not separate the two sides so the match went to a penalty shoot-out, which City won 4-3. Goalkeeper Maik Taylor made the vital save to keep out Craig Woodman's effort and send Blues into the next round where they would meet Aston Villa.

MAIK TAYLOR

SATURDAY 20th OCTOBER 1894

Freddie Wheldon scored the first penalty in Blues history as Aston Villa were held to a 2-2 draw at Muntz Street.

SATURDAY 20th OCTOBER 1923

Blues legend Joe Bradford scored just seven minutes into his England debut. Despite the early lead England lost the Home Championships match 2-1 to Ireland at Windsor Park in Belfast.

SATURDAY 20th OCTOBER 2001

Birmingham City blitzed Bradford City with four goals in 12 minutes as they made light of a lack of manager to win 4-0 at St Andrew's. Brazilian striker Marcelo scored three of the goals and laid on the other for Danny Sonner as Blues continued to look for a successor to Trevor Francis. Marcelo converted a Stan Lazaridis cross to open the scoring on 39 minutes before teeing up Sonner two minutes later. He tapped in a third goal just before the break and completed his hat-trick four minutes after the restart.

THURSDAY 20th OCTOBER 2011

A dramatic Chris Wood winner deep into stoppage time gave Blues victory over Club Brugge in Belgium. The home side had taken early lead through Joseph Akpala's low strike before David Murphy tapped in from Chris Burke's low cross to level the scores. Blues then lost Spanish defender Pablo Ibanez when he was knocked unconscious after clashing heads with Akpala. The incident visibly shook some of the Birmingham players and caused ten minutes to be added on. In the 9th minute of stoppage time Wood struck, firing in a Marlon King cross to send City to the top of Group H alongside Brugge.

MONDAY 20th OCTOBER 2014

Manager Lee Clark was sacked after a dismal run that had left the team just a point clear of the relegation places. Clark had led Blues to 12th place in the Championship in his first season in charge but relegation had only been avoided on the final day. City's home form had been dismal under Clark with only one win in over 12 months and a 1-0 defeat to Bolton Wanderers at St Andrew's proved the final straw.

SATURDAY 21st OCTOBER 1893

Small Heath's first league meeting with Woolwich Arsenal turned into a lop-sided affair as Blues ran out 4-1 winners at Muntz Street. Two goals from Freddie Wheldon and one apiece from Jack Hallam and Tommy Hands sealed a comfortable win for the home team.

SATURDAY 21st OCTOBER 1972

Welsh international defender John Roberts scored a debut goal to earn Blues a point in a 1-1 draw against Southampton. Roberts, who had arrived at St Andrew's from Arsenal, went on to play another 78 matches for Birmingham City but never scored another goal for the club.

SATURDAY 22nd OCTOBER 1994

Right-wing Mark Ward scored at both ends in Birmingham City's 2-1 victory over Brentford. Peter Shearer gave Blues the lead at Griffin Park and Ward made it two for the visitors on 70 minutes. He inadvertently pulled a goal back for the home side 13 minutes later but fortunately it turned out to be a mere consolation for the Bees.

SATURDAY 22nd OCTOBER 2011

Former Blues midfielder Robbie Savage broke his nose while performing a knee slide on BBC Television's *Strictly Come Dancing*. Despite the injury Savage continued in the competition eventually finishing in sixth place. Savage joined Blues from Leicester City in 2002 and helped the side maintain its Premier League status over the next two seasons. He made 88 appearances and scored 12 goals in all competitions for Blues.

WEDNESDAY 23rd OCTOBER 1957

Eddie Brown's 2nd-minute strike set the tone for a rollercoaster first leg of the Inter-Cities Fairs Cup semi-final against Barcelona at St Andrew's. The visitors fought back to take the lead through Justo Tejada and Evaristo only for two goals in two minutes to restore Blues' advantage. Bryan Orritt levelled for Blues and Peter Murphy put them back in front. Barca equalised once more through Paraguayan striker Eulogio Martinez before Murphy's second goal of the night made it 4-3 to City.

TUESDAY 23rd OCTOBER 1990

Blues registered a record eighth consecutive draw as they were held 1-1 by Crewe Alexandra in a Third Division fixture. Midfielder Nigel Gleghorn was the City scorer at Gresty Road.

SATURDAY 24th OCTOBER 1908

Birmingham City's Walter Corbett won an Olympic gold medal as part of the triumphant Great Britain team at the 1908 Olympics in London. The GB side won the football final beating Denmark 2-0 at White City thanks to goals from Fred Chapman and Vivian Woodward. In goal for the Great Britain side that won Olympic gold was Horace Bailey, who would join Blues two years later.

WEDNESDAY 24th OCTOBER 1962

Wales international Ken Leek scored Birmingham City's first two away goals of the season to give Blues a 2-0 win over Wolverhampton Wanderers. Leek's strikes were the first goals Birmingham had managed on their travels during the 1962/63 season and earned City their first win at Molineux in over 40 years.

SATURDAY 24th OCTOBER 1964

Blues debutant Geoff Vowden took just 16 minutes to score his first Birmingham City goal with the opener against Blackpool at St Andrew's. Blues went on to register a comfortable 3-0 victory over the Tangerines with further first-half goals from Ken Leek and Stan Lynn, who converted a penalty. Vowden had signed from Nottingham Forest in a £25,000 deal. The Barnsley-born striker scored 10 goals in his first season with City. He scored over 20 goals in each of the following three seasons in Birmingham and was top scorer in two of those years. Vowden scored 94 goals in total over 253 Blues appearances in all competitions before moving to Aston Villa for £12,000 in 1971.

SATURDAY 25th OCTOBER 1941

A crowd of 25,000 were at St Andrew's to see the ground host a wartime international between England and Wales. England won the match 2-1 thanks to goals from Reading inside-forward Maurice Edelston and Sheffield United's Jimmy Hagan.

SATURDAY 25th OCTOBER 2014

Five days after the sacking of manager Lee Clark the Blues fell to their worst league defeat in over half a century as promotion-chasing Bournemouth hit eight goals. Brett Pitman gave the visitors the lead after just three minutes and four minutes later Blues were down to ten men as David Edgar saw red. Marc Pugh grabbed a hat-trick, Tokelo Rantie got two and Matt Ritchie scored in an 8-0 rout. Paul Caddis had a penalty saved by Artur Boruc, on a day when nothing went right for the managerless Blues.

WEDNESDAY 26th OCTOBER 1960

Blues progressed to the quarter-finals of the 1960/61 Inter-Cities Fairs Cup final with a 2-1 win over Ujpesti Dosza in the Hungarian capital Budapest thanks to two late goals. Birmingham led the tie 3-2 from the home leg but Hungarian international Ferenc Szusza levelled the aggregate scores with a 63rd-minute strike. Billy Rudd restored the visitors' advantage with three minutes left to play and Jimmy Singer's 90th minute goal made it 5-3 over the two legs.

SATURDAY 27th OCTOBER 1990

Birmingham City's 12-match unbeaten run came to a shuddering halt as ex-Blues striker Wayne Clarke inflicted their first defeat of the season. Clarke scored a hat-trick as Shrewsbury Town beat Blues 4-1 at Gay Meadow. Town midfielder Paul Wimbleton added the home side's fourth goal in the 82nd minute and Dennis Bailey scored a consolation for the visitors 60 seconds later.

WEDNESDAY 27th OCTOBER 1999

Two goals in three minutes from debutant Marcelo rescued a point for Blues at Queens Park Rangers. Birmingham were trailing 2-0 to Rob Steiner and Chris Kiwomya goals at Loftus Road when the Brazilian struck. He scored his first City goal in the 74th minute and repeated the trick in the 76th minute to secure a draw in this First Division fixture. Marcelo, who had arrived at St Andrew's earlier in that month in a £500,000 deal from Sheffield United, went on to score 27 goals in 93 appearances for Blues.

SUNDAY 28th OCTOBER 1984

Obafemi Martins was born in Lagos, Nigeria. The striker played for Italian sides Reggiana and Internazionale, where he won two Serie A titles, before moving to England with Newcastle United. He also won caps for his country and enjoyed a short spell at Blues on loan from Russian side Rubin Kazan. He played in six matches for City, scoring two goals, and will forever be remembered by Blues fans as the man who came off the bench to score the winner in the 2011 League Cup final against Arsenal.

SATURDAY 28th OCTOBER 2006

Birmingham City skipper Damien Johnson suffered a broken jaw after being elbowed by West Bromwich Albion's Paul Robinson, in the dying moments of the West Midlands derby. Blues boss Steve Bruce said, 'I like Robinson as a player. I think he is the best full-back in the Championship but there is no need to mount a challenge like that.' Gary McSheffrey scored twice to give Blues victory at St Andrew's. McSheffrey top scored for City with 13 goals as they finished second in the Championship.

SATURDAY 29th OCTOBER 1898

Birmingham-born Billy Walton scored a hat-trick as Small Heath trounced Welsh side Chirk 8-0 in the third qualifying round of the FA Cup. Jimmy Inglis and Walter Abbott scored two goals each with Alex Leake adding another. Walton was born in Hockley Green and joined Small Heath as a 17-year-old from Hockley Belmont. He was part of a potent Small Heath attack along with Frank Mobley and Fred Wheldon. The trio scored over 100 goals in two seasons together between 1892 and 1894. Walton was a lifelong Blues fan attending the 1886 FA Cup semi-final against West Brom as well as both of Birmingham City's FA Cup Final appearances.

SATURDAY 29th OCTOBER 1949

Charles Field died in Hayes, Middlesex, aged 70. The forward, who was known as Oakey, joined Small Heath from Sheffield United in January 1902. He played a key role in Blues' promotion campaign of 1902/03 and scored 15 goals in 89 appearances for Small Heath.

MONDAY 29th OCTOBER 1962

Birmingham City continued their progress towards the League Cup trophy as Barrow were dispatched 5-1 in a second round replay. Ken Leek set Blues on course for victory with a goal after just six minutes. The home side cut loose in the second half with a Jimmy Harris double and a goal from Robin Stubbs with Barrow's Brian Arrowsmith scoring an own goal.

SATURDAY 29th OCTOBER 1966

A 1-1 Second Division draw with Blackburn Rovers was livened up by the debut of the club's new mascot Beau Brummie. Blues had decided to create a mascot following the success of World Cup Willie earlier in the year. Beau's first appearance was in the matchday programme with the image also being used on merchandise. Beau was brought to life by a furry costume in 1997 and has since helped to lead the team out and cheer them on. On the pitch at St Andrew's the Blues secured a point against Rovers thanks to a Malcolm Beard strike.

SATURDAY 30th OCTOBER 1920

Blues' winning streak continued with a convincing 4-0 victory over Sheffield Wednesday. Johnny Crosbie, Joe Lane, Harry Hampton and Jackie Whitehouse were all on target as City made it three league wins in succession, a sequence that would eventually stretch to ten, as a charge to the Second Division title began to gain momentum.

SUNDAY 30th OCTOBER 2016

Former Blues manager Steve Bruce returned to St Andrew's as Aston Villa boss for the first Second City derby in five years. Villa were unbeaten since Bruce had taken charge and took the lead on 29 minutes through Gary Gardner's looping header. Three good chances fell to Birmingham striker Clayton Donaldson, including a header that the home side were convinced had crossed the line, but he was unable to make any of them count. Instead it was midfielder David Davis who levelled with a low drive after 71 minutes to make it 1-1. Blues manager Gary Rowett said, 'I was very pleased to get back into it after dominating the majority of it. The atmosphere was electric.'

SATURDAY 31st OCTOBER 1885

Forward Eddy Stanley scored Small Heath's first ever competitive hat-trick as he bagged four of Blues' nine goals against Burton Wanderers in an FA Cup first round tie. Small Heath won the match 9-2 with Thomas Davenport scoring twice while Arthur James, Robert Evetts and Harry Morris were all on target for Blues.

SATURDAY 31st OCTOBER 1931

Blues outside-left Ernie Curtis scored twice for Wales in a 3-2 defeat to Scotland in a Home Championships match at the Racecourse Ground in Wrexham. Curtis won three caps for Wales and scored three goals for his country. He had joined Birmingham City from Cardiff City in 1927 having won the FA Cup with the Bluebirds earlier that year. Curtis returned to Wembley Stadium with Blues for the 1931 FA Cup Final, but this time finished on the losing side. The Welshman scored 53 goals in 182 Blues appearances before returning to Cardiff City in 1934.

WEDNESDAY 31st OCTOBER 1956

German champions Borussia Dortmund were the visitors for a special friendly that marked the opening of the floodlights at St Andrew's. Bryan Orritt scored twice and Alex Govan grabbed Blues' third goal in a 3-3 draw.

MONDAY 31st OCTOBER 1960

A Mike Hellawell goal was enough to clinch a 1-0 victory in Birmingham City's first ever League Cup match. Blues travelled to Bradford Park Avenue for the second round tie.

TUESDAY 31st OCTOBER 2000

Blues stunned Premier League Tottenham Hotspur with three first-half goals at White Hart Lane. Dele Adebola opened the scoring from a Stan Lazaridis cross and then doubled the visitors' lead with a superb solo effort. Marc Burchill made it 3-0 on the stroke of half-time as he applied the finishing touch to Martin Grainger's 40-yard run and cross. Although Darren Anderton pulled a goal back for Spurs the Blues were rarely troubled as they moved a step closer to the League Cup final in Cardiff.

BIRMINGHAM CITY
On This Day

NOVEMBER

SATURDAY 1st NOVEMBER 1941

Winston Foster was born in South Yardley, Birmingham. The defender made his Blues debut as a 19-year-old in 1961 and played in the first leg of the Inter-Cities Fairs Cup against Roma later that year. After deputising for centre-half Trevor Smith for three seasons, he took over the role in 1964 and was Blues' first choice for the next two years. Smith played in 169 Birmingham matches in all competitions, and scored two goals, before moving to Plymouth Argyle in 1969.

TUESDAY 1st NOVEMBER 1994

Midfielder Jonathan Hunt became the first Blues player to score a league hat-trick in over nine years when his treble helped Birmingham City demolish Crewe Alexandra 5-0. The visitors had conceded seven goals in their previous match and were not able to muster much improvement against a rampant City side, despite striker Ashley Ward testing Blues keeper Ian Bennett early on. Winger Louie Donowa teed up the first of Hunt's two first-half strikes before making it 3-0 with a fine solo effort. Steve Claridge scored from a Jose Dominguez cross then Hunt claimed the matchball with a strike in the final minute.

SATURDAY 2nd NOVEMBER 1901

Inside-forward Walter Wigmore's goal was enough to give Small Heath a 1-0 victory over Bury in a First Division match at Muntz Street. Unfortunately Blues would only win one of their next 11 matches as they began sliding towards a 17th place finish, resulting in relegation back to the Second Division after just one season in the top flight.

SATURDAY 3rd NOVEMBER 1979

Fulham's Kevin Lock scored at both ends as the Londoners were beaten 4-2 at Craven Cottage. The result was revenge for Blues' opening day loss at St Andrew's. Archie Gemmill set them on their way with a 12th minute penalty after Don Givens had been fouled. Fulham levelled through Gordon Davies but Givens struck back before Lock put the ball past his own keeper. Lock then converted a spot kick for Fulham before Givens completed the win with a 68th minute strike as Blues' promotion push continued.

THURSDAY 3rd NOVEMBER 2011

Birmingham City kept up the pace in Group H of the Europa League after battling back from two goals down to earn a point against Club Brugge. The Belgian side took the lead when Thomas Meunier rifled home from a corner and doubled their lead when Joseph Akpala side-footed past Colin Doyle. Jean Beausejour pulled a goal back in the second half after Brugge failed to clear Nikola Zigic's effort. And substitute Marlon King levelled the scores from the penalty spot following Ryan Donk's foul on Beausejour.

TUESDAY 4th NOVEMBER 1941

Johnny McMillan died in Derby aged 70. The Scottish inside-left signed for Small Heath from Leicester Fosse in January 1901. He played in 13 league matches of the 1900/01 season, scoring 10 goals, to help Blues gain promotion with a second-place finish in the Second Division. Although injuries hampered his progress over the next two seasons, McMillan still managed 25 goals in 52 Small Heath appearances before joining Bradford City, who he captained in the club's first ever Football League match in 1903.

TUESDAY 4th NOVEMBER 1986

A crowd of just 821 were at St Andrew's to see Birmingham City's first run in the Full Members Cup come to an end with a 3-2 defeat to Charlton Athletic. Striker Dave Geddis scored for Blues with Charlton's Peter Shirtliff adding an own goal.

SATURDAY 5th NOVEMBER 1887

The first competitive meeting between Small Heath and Aston Villa took place at Wellington Road in the second round of the FA Cup with the hosts winning 4-0.

SATURDAY 5th NOVEMBER 1977

Sir Alf Ramsey's first match as Blues boss ended in a 2-1 win over Wolverhampton Wanderers. Trevor Francis scored the first goal for the new manager with Terry Hibbitt getting Blues' winner four minutes after Martin Patching had equalised. Earlier, City keeper Jim Montgomery had saved a penalty from Wolves' Kenny Hibbitt, brother of the scorer of Birmingham's opening goal.

SATURDAY 5th NOVEMBER 1994

Blues finally managed a win at Gay Meadow on their 11th visit to Shrewsbury Town's ground. Gary Bull gave the visitors the lead after just four minutes and Jonathan Hunt added a second after the interval to make it 2-0.

SATURDAY 6th NOVEMBER 1971

Record signing Bob Hatton scored his first Blues goal just 19 minutes into his home debut against Orient. Hatton had joined Birmingham from Carlisle United the previous month in an £82,500 deal. He completed a brilliant attacking trio with Bob Latchford and Trevor Francis, which would fire the club to promotion. Despite his late start, Hatton scored 15 league goals in his first season while Latchford, who got the second goal in the 2-0 win over Orient, top scored with 23.

MONDAY 7th NOVEMBER 1864

Chris Charsley was born in Leicester. The goalkeeper made 80 appearances for Small Heath in the Football Alliance, Football League and FA Cup. Charsley was part of the Small Heath side that won the inaugural Second Division title and helped the club win promotion the following season. He was also the first Small Heath player to win an England cap.

SATURDAY 8th NOVEMBER 1919

Centre forward James Short scored both goals in a 2-0 victory over Wolverhampton Wanderers in front of 30,000 at St Andrew's. Short had arrived from Notts County and scored on his debut earlier in the month. The striker would find the target 10 times in just 16 appearances for Blues before he moved to Watford.

WEDNESDAY 9th NOVEMBER 1988

Birmingham City suffered their worst ever defeat to Aston Villa as they were trounced 6-0 in a Full Members Cup match at Villa Park.

SATURDAY 10th NOVEMBER 1894

Small Heath's first Football League meeting with West Bromwich Albion ended in a 4-1 defeat. Tommy Hands scored Blues' consolation goal at Stoney Lane.

SATURDAY 10th NOVEMBER 1945

Tommy Lawton scored twice for Chelsea but could not prevent his new club going down 3-2 to Birmingham in a wartime fixture at Stamford Bridge. Lawton twice levelled for the home side after Welsh international Wilson Jones had twice put Birmingham in front. An Arthur Turner penalty won the match for the visitors.

SATURDAY 10th NOVEMBER 1990

Blues beat Chester City 1-0 despite finishing the match with midfielder Nigel Gleghorn in goal, after a 57th minute injury to goalkeeper Martin Thomas. City held on and a late strike from wing Robert Hopkins snatched the points. The game was played at Macclesfield Town's Moss Rose ground as Chester were still waiting for plans for the Deva Stadium to be approved after being evicted from Sealand Road.

TUESDAY 11th NOVEMBER 1958

Goals from Bunny Larkin and Brian Taylor secured Birmingham's passage into the quarter-finals of the Inter-Cities Fairs Cup. Blues beat the Cologne XI 2-0 at St Andrew's to complete a 4-2 aggregate victory over the Germans.

WEDNESDAY 11th NOVEMBER 1959

Belgian side Union Saint-Gilloise were beaten 4-2 at St Andrew's to send Blues through to the final of the Inter-Cities Fairs Cup final for the first time. Johnny Gordon scored twice with further goals from Bunny Larkin and Harry Hooper. The score was a repeat of the away leg putting Birmingham through 8-4 on aggregate.

SATURDAY 11th NOVEMBER 1978

Blues smashed five past Manchester United to record their first win of the season. City were rock bottom of the First Division having lost eight of their past nine matches and things did not look good when future Birmingham boss Lou Macari laid on the opening goal for United's Joe Jordan. However, three goals in the space of 15 minutes turned the match City's way with Kevin Dillon and Alan Buckley, twice, on target. Don Givens' header shortly after half-time extended the lead and in the closing stages Jimmy Calderwood made it 5-1.

SATURDAY 12th NOVEMBER 1898

Small Heath inflicted the heaviest defeat in Luton Town's history with a 9-0 thrashing at Muntz Street. Welsh half-back William Robertson led the rout with a hat-trick while Arthur Gardner scored twice. Future Blues manager Bob McRoberts, outside-right Jimmy Inglis, winger Sid Wharton and inside-left Walter Abbott scored a goal apiece.

SATURDAY 12th NOVEMBER 1960

Blues goalkeeper Johnny Schofield suffered a fractured skull whilst playing against Manchester United. Bryan Orritt took over temporarily in goal, but Schofield, who would later have a metal plate inserted in his head, courageously returned and finished the game for Blues who won 3-1. Wing-half Dick Neal gave Birmingham a first-half lead and two goals in four minutes through Johnny Gordon and Brian Taylor sealed the victory.

SATURDAY 13th NOVEMBER 1920

Percy Barton's spectacular long-range header helped Blues to a 4-1 victory over Wolverhampton Wanderers. Barton headed home from 35 yards out with Harry Hampton scoring twice and Joe Lane rounding off a convincing win as Blues' title charge continued.

WEDNESDAY 13th NOVEMBER 1957

Birmingham City lost by a solitary goal in the second leg of the Inter-Cities Fairs Cup semi-final against Barcelona in front of 60,000 at the Camp Nou Stadium. Blues were leading 4-3 from the first leg at St Andrew's a month earlier. They appeared to be heading for the final until Hungarian forward Laszlo Kubala levelled the tie in the 82nd minute by lobbing Gil Merrick who had strayed off his line. There was no away-goals rule so 30 minutes of extra time were played and when that failed to separate the two sides they met again for a play-off in neutral Switzerland.

SATURDAY 14th NOVEMBER 1896

Former Aston Villa star Denny Hodgetts scored his first Small Heath goal as Woolwich Arsenal were trashed 5-2 at Muntz Street. Debutant Charlie Hare, who had joined from Arsenal a few days earlier, was also on the score-sheet as were Tot Farnall, Billy Walton and William Robertson.

WEDNESDAY 14th NOVEMBER 1962

A last minute Jimmy Harris winner ensured that Blues continued their progress towards the League Cup final. The tie had appeared in the balance after Notts County came from two goals down to level match. Birmingham had led through a Bertie Auld goal and a Stan Lynn penalty at the break. But the Magpies struck back to make it 2-2 and Blues only avoided a second successive replay in the competition thanks to Harris' late effort.

TUESDAY 15th NOVEMBER 1955

George Morrall died in Birmingham aged 50. The Smethwick-born centre-half was a mainstay of Blues' defence for nine seasons after making his debut against Derby County in December 1927. He also was part of the Birmingham City team that played in the 1931 FA Cup Final. In total, Morrall played 266 times for Blues and scored six goals.

WEDNESDAY 15th NOVEMBER 1995

'The Battle of Ancona' took place as Blues' Anglo-Italian Cup tie descended into violence and chaos. Blues manager Barry Fry said his team were 'kicked, punched and spat at throughout the whole game.' Things got worse after the final whistle as a fracas in the tunnel ended with the Italian police confiscating the passports of Liam Daish and Michael Johnson.

SATURDAY 16th NOVEMBER 1974

Centre-forward Bob Hatton scored his 100th league goal as Birmingham City put four past high-flying Manchester City. The striker scored two against the Citizens and would finish the season as Blues' top scorer with 18 goals to his name in all competitions. Howard Kendall and Kenny Burns were also on target against Manchester City.

SATURDAY 17th NOVEMBER 1934

Welsh international Wilson Jones scored twice and Billy Guest once as Grimsby Town were beaten 3-2 in a First Division match at St Andrew's. Jones top scored for Blues with 17 goals during the 1934/35 season. The following year he was top scorer once again, improving his total to 20 for the campaign.

MONDAY 17th NOVEMBER 1980

Birmingham City's Joe Gallagher gained international honours for the only time as he played in England B's 1-0 victory over Australia on his home ground. There were 3,292 at St Andrew's to see Gallagher tee up Arsenal striker Alan Sunderland for the only goal of the game.

SATURDAY 18th NOVEMBER 1972

Birmingham City lifted their Victoria Ground hoodoo with a first away victory at Stoke in 13 attempts and over half a century. Two goals from Bob Latchford secured a rare win in Stoke despite former Blue Jimmy Greenhoff giving the hosts an early lead. Blues' previous victory at the Victoria Ground had come in November 1920.

SATURDAY 19th NOVEMBER 1898

Blues romped to their biggest ever FA Cup victory as Druids were dispatched 10-0 in the fourth qualifying round. Frank McRoberts grabbed a hat-trick while Walter Abbott and Jimmy Inglis scored a brace each. Arthur Gardner and Alex Leake scored one each while Druids added an own goal to complete their miserable afternoon. This was the second of a sequence of three FA Cup ties that saw 25 goals scored with none conceded.

SATURDAY 19th NOVEMBER 1960

Blues goalkeeper Colin Withers had a league debut to forget at White Hart Lane as City were hit for six by double-chasing Tottenham Hotspur. Spurs' Welsh international Cliff Jones and Terry Dyson scored twice each while John White added another and Bobby Smith converted a penalty. Despite the 6-0 drubbing Withers would go on to make over a 100 appearances for Birmingham.

MONDAY 19th NOVEMBER 2007

Wigan Athletic announced that Birmingham City's Steve Bruce would be joining them as manager. The Latics paid £3m in compensation for Bruce, who joined officially four days later. Bruce's six-year reign at St Andrew's had seen the club promoted to the Premier League twice but he left a side in freefall, which had only won one of its previous seven matches, and was heading for relegation.

STEVE BRUCE

WEDNESDAY 20th NOVEMBER 1929

Blues goalkeeper Harry Hibbs made his England debut in a 6-0 Home Championships thrashing of Wales at Stamford Bridge. Hibbs would go on to win another 24 England caps, the most by a player whilst at Birmingham City.

THURSDAY 21st NOVEMBER 1901

Ned Barkas was born in Gateshead, Tyne and Wear. The full-back won two league championships with Huddersfield Town before becoming Leslie Knighton's first signing as Birmingham City manager in 1928. Barkas made 288 appearances in nine seasons with Blues, scored nine goals, and was part of the 1931 FA Cup Final team.

WEDNESDAY 21st NOVEMBER 1990

Birmingham-born striker John Gayle joined Blues from Wimbledon in a £175,000 deal. Gayle is best remembered for the two spectacular strikes that helped Blues win the Leyland-DAF Cup final at Wembley in 1991.

SATURDAY 21st NOVEMBER 2009

Lee Bowyer's 16th minute strike secured a 1-0 victory over Fulham in the Premier League. The starting line-up of Joe Hart, Stephen Carr, Liam Ridgewell, Roger Johnson, Scott Dann, Lee Bowyer, Seb Larsson, Barry Ferguson, James McFadden, Cameron Jerome and Christian Benitez would stay together for the next 11 matches setting a Premier League record. Blues only lost once during that run with seven victories and four draws helping them towards a 9th place finish, the club's best since the formation of the Premier League.

SATURDAY 22nd NOVEMBER 1930

Blues legend Joe Bradford scored his seventh and final England goal in his last appearance for the national side. Bradford was winning the last of his 12 England caps when he scored the fourth goal in a 4-0 rout of Wales at the Racecourse Ground, Wrexham. Earlier in the match Blues goalkeeper Harry Hibbs had saved a Fred Keenor penalty to preserve England's clean sheet.

SATURDAY 22nd NOVEMBER 2003

The crowd of 29,588 that saw Blues go down 3-0 to Arsenal in the Premier League remains a record for St Andrew's since it became an all-seater stadium.

SATURDAY 23rd NOVEMBER 1935

Welsh international centre-forward Wilson Jones scored both Blues goals as the Second City derby against Aston Villa ended in a 2-2 stalemate. The crowd of 60,250 watching at St Andrew's remains a league record for the ground. Jones' total of 20 goals made him top scorer for Blues for a second successive season.

WEDNESDAY 23rd NOVEMBER 1960

A meagre crowd of 2,500 were in attendance to see Blues take on Boldklub Copenhagen. It is the lowest crowd ever to watch a European match involving Birmingham City, but those at Parken in Copenhagen were treated to an eight-goal classic. Blues looked set to run away with the tie, leading 4-1 after 61 minutes thanks to a brace of goals each from Johnny Gordon and Bryan Singer. However, the home side fought back with three late goals to level the tie at 4-4.

SATURDAY 23rd NOVEMBER 1985

Goals from Liverpool strikers Ian Rush and Paul Walsh condemned Blues to a record-equalling eighth consecutive league defeat as they went down 2-0 to the double-chasing Reds at St Andrew's. The poor run was broken by a draw in City's next match against Arsenal, but four more losses followed that result as Blues headed for the relegation trapdoor.

SATURDAY 24th NOVEMBER 1973

Blues striker Bob Latchford scored his second hat-trick in four days getting all three goals in a 3-0 First Division victory over Leicester City at St Andrew's. The treble continued a hot streak for Latchford who made it eight goals from three Blues matches.

SATURDAY 24th NOVEMBER 1979

Birmingham City striker Keith Bertschin scored all three Blues goals in a 3-2 win over Luton Town. The former England Under-21 international had joined Blues from Ipswich Town two years earlier in a £100,000 deal. Despite suffering two broken legs in his four-year spell at St Andrew's the striker still managed to clock up 144 appearances and scored 44 goals for City.

TUESDAY 25th NOVEMBER 1975

Scottish giants Celtic visited St Andrew's for a special friendly match to celebrate Birmingham City's centenary. The visitors boasted a team that included Kenny Dalglish and Danny McGrain as well as European Cup winner Bobby Lennox. They also had former Blue Peter Latchford in goal. Birmingham won the match 1-0 through a Peter Withe goal with Steve Smith saving a Pat McCluskey penalty.

SATURDAY 25th NOVEMBER 1978

Argentine World Cup winner Alberto Tarantini scored his one and only Blues goal to earn Birmingham a 1-1 draw against Bristol City.

SATURDAY 25th NOVEMBER 2006

Blues striker DJ Campbell scored with his first touch after coming on at Turf Moor as City's excellent away form continued. Chris McCann gave Burnley an early lead, which was cancelled out by a Nicklas Bendtner tap in. Steve Bruce sent Campbell into the action on 82 minutes and 60 seconds later he pounced on a mistake by Clarets keeper Brian Jensen to earn Birmingham a fifth successive win on the road. Bruce said, 'It was inspired. We wanted to put substitute DJ Campbell up the top and we didn't want to break up Nicklas Bendtner and Gary McSheffrey. We decided to push on another offensive player because we believed we could go on to win the match. It's been frustrating for DJ so I'm delighted for the kid.'

SATURDAY 26th NOVEMBER 1898

Small Heath's goal-scoring rampage continued at Muntz Street as they thrashed Darwen 8-0. Inside-left Walter Abbott starred for Blues with five goals, including a penalty. Inside-forward Arthur Gardner added two goals with William Robertson also on target against the Lancashire team. The result continued a run of four games, two in the league and two in the FA Cup, that saw Small Heath score 35 goals without reply on home soil.

SUNDAY 26th NOVEMBER 1944

Geoff Anderson was born in Sheerness, Kent. The right-wing played one match for Birmingham City in 1964 before moving to Mansfield Town.

TUESDAY 26th NOVEMBER 1957

Birmingham City met Barcelona at the St Jakob Stadium in Basel, Switzerland in the Inter-Cities Fairs Cup. The original home and away ties failed to separate the teams and so they met for a play-off on neutral ground. Once again it was a late goal from Laszlo Kubala that decided the match. The Hungarian forward's strike had levelled the tie at the Camp Nou and he struck to send Barca through to the final where they thrashed a London XI 8-2 on aggregate. Earlier Peter Murphy had equalised for Blues after Brazilian striker Evaristo had given Barca the lead.

SATURDAY 27th NOVEMBER 1909

There were only 1,000 spectators at St Andrew's to see Blues go down 2-1 to Blackpool in a Second Division match. Fred Chapple got the City goal in front of a crowd that remains the equal lowest ever to witness a senior fixture at the ground.

SATURDAY 27th NOVEMBER 1954

Birmingham City registered the first big win of Arthur Turner's managerial reign with a 7-2 thrashing of Port Vale at St Andrew's. Inside-left Peter Murphy led the rout with a hat-trick, Welsh international Noel Kinsey scored twice while Eddie Brown and Alex Govan chipped in with a goal apiece. Turner had taken over at the struggling Blues earlier in the month and would lead them to the Second Division title by the end of a season, during which the team scored 98 league goals.

WEDNESDAY 28th NOVEMBER 2007

Former Scotland manager Alex McLeish was named as the new Birmingham City manager following the departure of Steve Bruce. McLeish said, 'I have always harboured a desire to manage in the Premier League and I am really excited about the challenge.' Although McLeish was unable to save Blues from relegation he led them straight back to the Premier League. He followed that with a 9th place finish in 2010, City's highest league place in over half a century, and a League Cup triumph the next season. However, that trophy could not prevent his side dropping out of the top flight and although the club stood by McLeish he left for local rivals Aston Villa in controversial circumstances.

SATURDAY 29th NOVEMBER 1913

Blues lost 2-1 to Grimsby Town in a match that was overshadowed by a bribery scandal. Birmingham captain Frank Womack had been offered 55 guineas to fix the match as a draw. Womack reported the incident to the police and the culprit was arrested and charged.

SATURDAY 29th NOVEMBER 1924

Striker Joe Bradford scored the first of his record 13 Blues hat-tricks as Liverpool were well beaten in a First Division clash. The final score at St Andrew's was 5-2 with Blues' other goals coming from Ernie Islip and Percy Barton.

SATURDAY 30th NOVEMBER 1918

Forward Joby Godfrey scored a hat-trick as Blues thrashed Barnsley 7-0 to record their biggest victory during World War One. Billy Walker scored twice against the Tykes with Jackie Whitehouse and guest player George Hunter also on target. Godfrey scored 25 times and Whitehouse 17 as Blues clocked up 85 goals and finished second in the Midland Section of the wartime competition.

SATURDAY 30th NOVEMBER 1968

Birmingham-born striker Phil Summerill set the record for the fastest hat-trick in Blues history when he hit the back of the net three times in just seven minutes against Hull City. Birmingham had thrown away a two-goal lead at St Andrew's when Summerill struck. Goals in the 72nd, 77th and 79th minutes eased Blues to a 5-2 win. Goals from Fred Pickering and Jimmy Greenhoff had given City a 2-0 lead but Hull struck back twice. However, the visitors were only on terms for a minute before Summerill went on his goal-scoring spree.

WEDNESDAY 30th NOVEMBER 2011

Birmingham City's Europa League campaign suffered a major setback as they lost 1-0 to Portuguese side Braga. Nikola Zigic missed a penalty for Blues before Hugo Viana's shot deflected in off Curtis Davies for the only goal of the game.

BIRMINGHAM CITY
On This Day

DECEMBER

SATURDAY 1st DECEMBER 1979

Striker Frank Worthington made his Blues league debut against his former club Leicester City. Worthington's presence in the Birmingham line-up could not stop his old side taking the points at St Andrew's with a 2-1 win. Joe Gallagher scored for Blues in the 75th minute but it proved too little, too late.

SATURDAY 2nd DECEMBER 1961

Forward Ken Leek marked his Blues debut with a goal in the first minute against Cardiff City. The Welsh international repeated the trick in the 19th minute and Mike Hellawell scored after the break, as the Bluebirds were comfortably dispatched 3-0.

SATURDAY 3rd DECEMBER 1881

Small Heath's first FA Cup run came to a shuddering halt in the second round, as they were thrashed 6-0 at Wednesbury Old Athletic.

MONDAY 3rd DECEMBER 1956

Welsh inside-forward Bryan Orritt scored after just three minutes to start the first game of European football played at St Andrew's in style. Further goals from Eddie Brown and Peter Murphy made it a comfortable 3-0 win for Blues over the Zagreb XI as the team's good start in the Inter-Cities Fairs Cup continued.

SATURDAY 4th DECEMBER 1976

Kenny Burns won a Triumph TR7 sports car for scoring his third, and Birmingham's sixth, goal at Leicester City. The prize was offered by Blues fan Paul Banks for the player who scored the sixth City goal in a match. The Scottish striker claimed it and promptly sold the car, so he could share the proceeds with his team-mates. Blues won 6-2 at an icy Filbert Street after their choice of footwear proved more suitable than the home team's. The visitors were 4-0 up by the break as Leicester failed to adapt to conditions with two goals from Burns plus strikes from Gary Emmanuel and Trevor Francis. A Dennis Rofe own goal made it five before Burns completed his hat-trick. Steve Kember and future Blue, Frank Worthington, scored two late consolation goals for the Foxes.

SATURDAY 5th DECEMBER 1953

Five goals were scored in a crazy 11-minute spell, as Everton were thrashed 5-1 at St Andrew's in the First Division. The score was 0-0 at the break but inside-left Peter Murphy broke the deadlock with a strike that opened the floodgates after 55 minutes. Within two minutes City were two up as Gordon Astall grabbed a goal before Everton replied through John Willie Parker. Cyril Trigg made it 3-1 in the 65th minute and 60 seconds later Astall scored his second of the match. Everton defender Tommy Clinton completed the scoring with an own goal.

SATURDAY 5th DECEMBER 1970

Malcolm Beard's 405th and final Blues game ended in disappointment when he was sent off at Millwall. City went down 2-1 at Cold Blow Lane with Phil Summerill scoring Blues' consolation goal. Beard, who scored 33 goals, made 403 starts and three substitute appearances in all competitions for Birmingham City, putting him seventh on the all-time list.

SATURDAY 6th DECEMBER 1890

Charlie Short and Jack Hallam scored the goals as Small Heath beat Wednesbury Old Athletic in the FA Cup. However, it transpired that Short, who had also played in the first round victory against Hednesford Town, was not properly registered for the competition. A breach of the rules that led to Small Heath's disqualification from the FA Cup for the 1890/91 season. One local press report called the error, 'quite the most egregious blunder which has been perpetrated in football circles this season.'

WEDNESDAY 7th DECEMBER 1960

Blues recorded their biggest ever European win as Boldklub Copenhagen were put to the sword 5-0 in the second leg of the 1960-61 Inter-Cities Fairs Cup. The two sides were locked together at 4-4 after the first leg but Robin Stubbs gave Blues the lead after just four minutes. Three goals in five minutes early in the second half ended the match as a contest with Jimmy Harris getting the first before Mike Hellawell and Jimmy Bloomfield both benefitted from goalkeeping blunders. Stubbs completed the rout in the 67th minute.

THURSDAY 7th DECEMBER 1961

Blues tumbled out of the Inter-Cities Fairs Cup after a bad-tempered match with Espanyol. Bertie Auld's goal gave Birmingham a 1-0 victory on the night but the tie finished 5-3 to the Spaniards. Auld and Jimmy Harris were both sent off while Espanyol also finished with nine men.

SATURDAY 8th DECEMBER 1888

Brothers Will and Ted Devey scored four goals each as Burton Wanderers were thrashed 9-0 in the fourth qualifying round of the FA Cup. Charlie Short's goal completed the rout to set up a meeting with West Bromwich Albion in the first round proper.

TUESDAY 9th DECEMBER 1969

Simon Sturridge was born in Birmingham. The 5ft 5in striker progressed through the youth system at St Andrew's before making his first team debut in 1988. He played in over 180 Blues matches scoring 30 goals, which included City's opener in the Leyland-DAF Cup final against Tranmere Rovers at Wembley.

SATURDAY 10th DECEMBER 1898

Small Heath recorded the club's biggest ever win over Burslem Port Vale, handing out a 7-0 drubbing in the 5th qualifying round of the FA Cup. It took the team's goal tally to 25 in three FA Cup matches that season, after Chirk had been beaten 8-0 and Druids thrashed 10-0 in the previous rounds. Walter Abbott was Vale's main tormentor with a hat-trick while Bob McRoberts, Arthur Gardner, Sid Wharton and Jimmy Inglis all contributed a goal to the win.

FRIDAY 10th DECEMBER 1993

Former Barnet and Southend United manager Barry Fry was given the job at St Andrew's following the departure of Terry Cooper the previous month. Fry, who was a larger than life character with a colourful turn of phrase, could not prevent relegation to the third tier. However, he led the side straight back the following season by completing the lower league double of Second Division title and Football League Trophy. Fry held the reigns at St Andrew's for two and a half eventful years.

SATURDAY 11th DECEMBER 1954

Blues recorded their biggest League win of the 20th Century as Liverpool were thrashed 9-1 in a Second Division clash at St Andrew's. Birmingham had put seven past Port Vale in their previous home match and wasted little time scoring more goals as Jackie Lane gave them the lead in just 42 seconds. Eddie Brown scored a hat-trick, Gordon Astall and Peter Murphy grabbed a brace while Alex Govan scored one. The final score made it 16 goals in two games on Blues' own pitch as they headed towards the title and promotion. The result remains Liverpool's worst defeat in all competitions.

TUESDAY 11th DECEMBER 1962

Blues received a helping hand from Manchester City as they ran up their biggest win in the League Cup. Own goals from Bill Leivers and Cliff Sear gave Birmingham a two-goal lead that Stan Lynn extended to three before half-time. Blues added three more goals late on through Ken Leek, a Lynn penalty and Bertie Auld to make it 6-0 as they headed towards the final.

TUESDAY 11th DECEMBER 2001

Less than two months after his departure, former Blues manager Trevor Francis returned to St Andrew's with his Crystal Palace side. In an ironic twist Francis' predecessor at Selhurst Park, Steve Bruce, who was on gardening leave, would be allowed to take the vacant Birmingham job immediately after this match had ended. On the pitch a Tommy Mooney penalty was enough to give Blues a 1-0 win.

SATURDAY 12th DECEMBER 1914

The Football Battalion was formed as part of the 'Pals' battalions scheme. The first volunteer for the battalion was Frank Buckley, who had played 56 matches as a defender for Blues during 1913/14. The battalion was part of the Middlesex Regiment and saw action at the Battle of the Somme in 1914 and Battle of Arras in 1917. Buckley, who rose to the rank of major during World War One, played for Aston Villa, both Manchester clubs and Derby County. After his playing career finished he moved into management with Blackpool and Wolves.

SUNDAY 12th DECEMBER 2004

A goalkeeping blunder by Aston Villa's Thomas Sorensen set Blues on the way to a 2-1 victory in the Second City derby. Sorensen let Clinton Morrison's speculative effort squirm through his fingers after just nine minutes to give City the lead at Villa Park. David Dunn slammed in a second goal from Damien Johnson's cross to cap a dominant first-half performance. Blues were the better side after the break, although they could not extend their lead, and Gareth Barry's late strike proved to be a mere consolation goal for Villa.

SATURDAY 13th DECEMBER 1997

It was the late, late show at St Andrew's with all three goals coming in a frantic finish. Visitors Manchester City looked like they had snatched victory when Georgian international Murtaz Shelia opened the scoring in the 88th minute, heading home unchallenged at a corner. In the final minute Blues sent Steve Bruce up for a free kick and although his header was saved Nick Forster followed up to score. Then in stoppage time Martyn O'Connor curled in a dramatic winning goal.

SATURDAY 14th DECEMBER 1968

Forward Fred Pickering scored after just 25 seconds to set Blues on course for victory against Bristol City. The former England international was on target again in the 14th minute as Birmingham ran out 2-0 winners at St Andrew's. Pickering, who scored a hat-trick on his England debut in 1964, had arrived from Everton a year earlier in a £50,000 deal. He scored 32 goals in 88 games for Blues before joining Blackpool.

WEDNESDAY 14th DECEMBER 2016

New owners Trillion Trophy Asia shocked Blues fans by sacking Gary Rowett and replacing him with former Italian international Gianfranco Zola, who had previously managed West Ham United and Watford. Rowett, who was a former Blues and Derby County defender, had returned to St Andrew's as manager in 2015 and rescued the club from the prospect of relegation. After a season of consolidation City looked poised to make a push for promotion with Rowett's side lying seventh in the Championship.

DAVID DUNN

SATURDAY 15th DECEMBER 1900

A rare Arthur Archer goal was enough to give Small Heath a 1-0 win over Middlesbrough at Linthorpe Road. The win made it 15 matches unbeaten at the start of the 1900/01 season, a run that laid the foundations for a second-place finish and promotion back to the First Division. Arthur, who was considered one of the toughest full-backs of the day, had signed for £50 from Burton Wanderers three years earlier. He played 170 matches for Small Heath and scored four goals.

SATURDAY 15th DECEMBER 1984

Striker Mick Harford was sold to First Division side Luton Town for £250,000. He had joined the club in March 1982 and scored the winning goal on his debut against Brighton & Hove Albion. Overall Harford scored 26 goals in 92 league appearances for Blues. In 1983 he scored the goal that preserved Birmingham's First Division status but sadly it only postponed the inevitable. The following season he was the club's top scorer as Blues suffered relegation.

THURSDAY 15th DECEMBER 2011

An Adam Rooney header made sure Blues completed their Europa League group matches with a 1-0 win over NK Maribor, but it was not enough to ensure progress in the competition. Nathan Redmond teed up Rooney's winner and struck the post himself as City dominated their defensive opponents without being able to add their score. However, Blues were relying on victory by Portuguese side Braga, who could only draw with Club Brugge, and they finished third in Group H.

SATURDAY 16th DECEMBER 1905

Freddie Wilcox's hat-trick inspired Blues to a 5-0 win over Nottingham Forest, but the goals turned out to be his last for the club. The inside-left didn't find the net again before moving to Middlesbrough. Roly Harper and Billy Jones scored Blues' other goals against Forest.

WEDNESDAY 16th DECEMBER 1992

Just 139 paying spectators saw Italian side Lucchese beat Blues 3-0 to end their Anglo-Italian Cup campaign.

SUNDAY 16th DECEMBER 2001

Birmingham City fell to a 2-1 defeat at Molineux in Steve Bruce's first match as manager of Blues. Alex Rae scored in the 66th minute for Wolves after goals for the home side's Nathan Blake and Blues' Brazilian striker Marcelo had kept the sides level at the break.

SATURDAY 17th DECEMBER 1892

Small Heath set the club record for the biggest win as Walsall Town Swifts were swept aside 12-0. Frank Mobley and Billy Walton each scored a hat-trick of goals while 'Diamond' Freddie Wheldon, Walter Hands and Jack Hallam all scored two in an emphatic victory.

SATURDAY 17th DECEMBER 1966

Geoff Vowden's 88th minute winner sealed a remarkable late comeback at St Andrew's and completed Blues' first league double over Wolverhampton Wanderers in 46 years. Wolves had led 2-0 at the break thanks to Dave Wagstaffe's close-range finish and Mike Bailey's 30-yard volley. The visitors held on to their two-goal advantage until the 68th minute when Vowden teed up former England striker Barry Bridges, who pulled a goal back with a fierce shot. Eight minutes later inside-forward Peter Bullock levelled the scores with a shot that cannoned in off the underside of the bar and with time running out Vowden struck the winning goal.

SATURDAY 18th DECEMBER 1920

A rare goal from centre-half Alec McClure was enough to see off the challenge of Leeds United with a 1-0 win. It was Blues' 10th consecutive victory.

SATURDAY 18th DECEMBER 1965

Inside-forward Ronnie Fenton became the first Blues substitute to score a goal when he put the icing on the cake of a 4-0 win over Bury with a strike in the final minute. Blues had overcome atrocious weather conditions to take command of the game with two goals from Dennis Thwaites and a Bobby Thompson volley. Thompson then had to take-over in goal after an injury to Jim Herriot. Fenton replaced him in attack and headed in the final goal from a Cammie Fraser cross.

SATURDAY 18th DECEMBER 2004

A convincing 4-0 win for Blues in the West Midlands derby left West Bromwich Albion rooted to the bottom of the Premier League at Christmas. Robbie Savage set City on course for victory with a penalty after Darren Purse had brought down Clinton Morrison in the area. Morrison picked himself up to add Blues' second before Emile Heskey's angled shot and Darren Anderton's deflected free-kick completed an easy win.

MONDAY 19th DECEMBER 1994

Blues manager Barry Fry broke the club record when he signed winger Rick Otto for £800,000 from his former club Southend United. Otto was unable to justify the size of the fee while at St Andrew's and had spells on loan at Charlton Athletic, Peterborough United and Notts County before being released from his contract in 1998. Almost half of the player's 45 league appearances for Blues came from the bench while he managed just eight goals in all competitions.

SATURDAY 20th DECEMBER 1952

Blues inside-left Peter Murphy's hot streak in front of goal continued as he scored in a 4-0 win over Rotherham United at St Andrew's. It was Murphy's ninth goal in as many games and he scored another two on Christmas Day as he headed for 26 goals for the campaign, a total that made him top scorer for the season. Also on target against Rotherham were Billy Wardle, Ted Purdon and Cyril Trigg with a penalty.

WEDNESDAY 20th DECEMBER 1995

Blues humbled Premier League Middlesbrough in the League Cup at St Andrew's. Birmingham had been unlucky not to beat Boro on Teeside in the original tie but made certain in the replay with Kevin Francis scoring twice in a 2-0 win. The giant striker latched on to Steve Claridge's pass and slammed the ball into the top corner after 11 minutes to open the scoring. Six minutes later Francis used his 6ft 7in height to send a powerful downward header past visiting keeper Gary Walsh. Blues boss Barry Fry said, 'I don't think anyone could deny that over 90 minutes we were the better team.'

SATURDAY 21st DECEMBER 1889

An injury ravaged Small Heath were forced to field a team of just nine players against Sheffield Wednesday and were punished with a record-equalling 9-1 defeat in the Football Alliance.

SATURDAY 22nd DECEMBER 1906

Blues said farewell to their Muntz Street ground in style with a 3-1 victory over Bury. The club's popularity had prompted the building of St Andrew's and their departure from their home for 29 years. The *Birmingham Daily Post* said, 'At the conclusion of the match the band played 'Auld Lang Syne', and the crowd silently left the ground which has been the home of the club for so many years and the scene of many brilliant victories and many heartbreaking defeats, and of an uphill struggle from which the club, thanks to the courage of the directors, has at length emerged triumphant.' Arthur Mounteney scored twice against Bury, including the final goal scored at the ground while half-back Walter Wigmore added another.

SATURDAY 23rd DECEMBER 1967

A second-half blitz saw five goals scored by five different players as Huddersfield Town were swept aside 6-1 at St Andrew's. The sides went into the break level at 1-1 after a header from future Blue Frank Worthington had cancelled out Fred Pickering's opening goal. But, four goals in 11 minutes put the contest beyond any doubt as Johnny Vincent, Graham Leggat and Geoff Vowden all found the back of the net before Pickering grabbed his second of the afternoon. A late Barry Bridges header completed the win.

THURSDAY 24th DECEMBER 1925

Noel Kinsey was born in Treorchy, Glamorgan. Manager Bob Brocklebank signed the Welsh international for Blues from Norwich City in 1953. However, it was under Arthur Turner that Kinsey enjoyed his best seasons with Birmingham City. He scored 14 goals as Blues took the Second Division title in 1955 and the following year added another 17 as the club reached its highest-ever finish in the league. Kinsey also scored at Wembley as Blues lost out to Manchester City in the 1956 FA Cup Final.

MONDAY 24th DECEMBER 1990

The 90th and final episode of BBC Television's *All Creatures Great and Small* was broadcast. The series, which ran for six years, was based on the books of vet Alf Wight, who wrote under the pseudonym James Herriot. Wight chose the name after watching an impressive performance from Blues keeper Jim Herriot in a televised match against Manchester United. Herriot was signed in 1965 for £17,500 from Middlesbrough. The goalkeeper made 212 appearances for Blues and won eight Scotland caps whilst a Birmingham City player.

TUESDAY 25th DECEMBER 1945

A gate of 30,000 were at St Andrew's to see if Blues could make it ten home wins in a row in the wartime Football League South. The crowd were not disappointed as Birmingham thrashed Leicester City 6-2 on their way to the title, which they clinched by pipping city rivals Aston Villa into second place on goal average. Wilson Jones scored twice and was unlucky not to get a hat-trick. Jock Mulraney claimed Blues' opener with further goals coming through Neil Dougall, Harold Bodle and Welsh international George Edwards.

MONDAY 25th DECEMBER 1916

An 8-2 drubbing at the hands of Rotherham County was Blues' worst defeat of wartime football during World War One.

WEDNESDAY 26th DECEMBER 1906

After ten months of work, which was directed by carpenter and Blues fan Harry Pumfrey, St Andrew's hosted its first football match. The work had seen a wasteland flattened out, stagnant pools drained, 10,000 square feet of turf laid and stands built. The result was a football stadium with an official capacity of 75,000. Finally, fans had to help clear overnight snow off the pitch so that Blues could host Middlesbrough for a hard-fought 0-0 draw.

MONDAY 26th DECEMBER 1955

Welsh striker Noel Kinsey scored his one and only Blues hat-trick as Birmingham City thrashed Everton 6-2. Eddie Brown scored twice and an Alex Govan strike completed the rout.

MONDAY 26th DECEMBER 1994

Defender David Howells became the oldest debutant in Blues history when he took the field against Cambridge United at St Andrew's. Howells was 36 years and 77 days old when he made the first of his two Birmingham City appearances, in a match that finished 1-1.

SUNDAY 26th DECEMBER 2004

Strictly Ice Dancing aired on BBC Television with former Blues keeper David Seaman, and his professional partner Zoia Birmingham, beating off the competition to win first prize. Seaman's achievement was all the more impressive as he was a late replacement for Paul Gascoigne and had only eight days to prepare for the competition.

TUESDAY 27th DECEMBER 1955

A day after hitting Everton for six, Birmingham City travelled to Goodison Park for the return fixture and were humbled 5-1 with Gordon Astall claiming Blues' consolation goal.

SATURDAY 27th DECEMBER 1980

Debutant goalkeeper Tony Coton saved a penalty kick with his first touch as a Blues player. Sunderland were the visitors when Joe Gallagher gave away the first-minute spot kick but Coton denied John Hawley from 12 yards. Birmingham went on to win the match 3-2 with goals from Archie Gemmill, Keith Bertschin and Frank Worthington.

MONDAY 27th DECEMBER 1982

Blues humbled Aston Villa's European Cup winners with a comprehensive 3-0 victory in the Second City derby. Midfielder Ian Handysides created the opening goal for Noel Blake before adding a second himself from a well-worked free-kick routine. Striker Mick Ferguson added a third as he bundled in an attempted clearance.

THURSDAY 28th DECEMBER 1916

Captain John Lauder of the Argyll and Sutherland Highlanders was killed in action during the Battle of the Somme. The death inspired his father, Sir Harry Lauder, to write the song 'Keep Right On To the End of the Road', which has since become an anthem for Blues fans.

WEDNESDAY 28th DECEMBER 1960

St Andrew's hosted the Springboks rugby union side as South Africa beat the Midland Counties 16-5 in a tour match.

SATURDAY 29th DECEMBER 1906

Inside-forward Benny Green had the honour of scoring Birmingham City's first ever goal at the newly-opened St Andrew's ground. Green was rewarded with the gift of a piano for christening the club's new home. He scored twice in the match and centre forward Billy Jones got another as Preston North End were comfortably despatched 3-0 to record Blues' first win at St Andrew's.

SUNDAY 30th DECEMBER 2007

Karren Brady was the castaway on BBC Radio 4's Desert Island Discs. Amongst the tracks she selected were Wham's 'Last Christmas', Abba's 'Dancing Queen' and Carole King's '(You Make Me Feel Like) A Natural Woman'. Brady's book choice was Jane Austen's *Pride & Prejudice* while her luxury item was her own pillow.

SATURDAY 31st DECEMBER 1977

Two late goals gave the scoreline a veneer of respectability as Birmingham City ended the year with a crazy nine-goal match against Chelsea. Keith Bertschin gave the home side an early lead at St Andrew's and, after the Londoners scored twice, Trevor Francis put them back on level terms. Chelsea extended their lead with goals either side of the break and made it 5-2 in the 79th minute. However, Francis scored his second of the game on 88 minutes and 60 seconds later Terry Hibbitt struck to make the final score 5-4 to the visitors.

SATURDAY 31st DECEMBER 1994

Barry Fry's rampant Blues team racked up the club's biggest win in 35 years as Blackpool were battered 7-1 at St Andrew's. The visitors took the lead through a Darren Bradshaw's 8th minute goal, although the same player gifted Blues an equaliser when he scored an own goal four minutes later. After that it was one-way traffic with Louie Donowa and Steve Claridge grabbing a brace each, while Kenny Lowe and George Parris were also on the scoresheet.

Bibliography

Birmingham City: The Complete Record
by Tony Matthews

Birmingham City Miscellany
by Tony Matthews

Today's the Day – Birmingham City Football Club
by Andrew Henry

Birmingham City: Modern Day Heroes
by Keith Dixon

Tom Ross: The Game's Gone
by Tom Ross

Birmingham City: 50 Greatest Matches
by Keith Dixon

Newspapers

Birmingham Mail
Sunday Mercury
Birmingham Daily Post
The Times
The Daily Telegraph
The Guardian

Websites

www.soccerbase.com
www.englandstats.com
www.cricketarchive.com